· ·

"How unfortunate that that war interrupted cycling. No Tour de France for four years and that in my best years. Damn, without that I could have won at least two more Tours!"

Philippe Thys

· ·

© 2014 Johan Van Win

**les
iles**

LES ILES PUBLISHERS
www.lesiles.be
lesilespublishers@gmail.com

ENGLISH VERSION :
ISBN: 9789491545733

ORIGINAL DUTCH-LANGUAGE VERSION:
ISBN: 978-94-91545-15-3
WD: 2014/12.833/18

Photos: Les Iles Archive, WIEMU Roeselare, Belga, BNF Gallica, Presse Sports, Sportimonium, Jammart, Daniel Lebrun Archive, Johan Van Win Archive.Design: Gunter

Segers - www.guntersegers.be

PHILIPPE THYS

JOHAN VAN WIN

THE FORGOTTEN THREE-TIME
WINNER OF THE TOUR DE FRANCE

Introduction

Altitude 100

Every year someone or something of interest turns 100. Some years ago it was the turn of the 100th edition of the Tour de France. Anniversaries that get a media retrospective are beyond counting. Historiography can be very selective. Only immortal platitudes get a refresher. Repetitive complacency too often takes over from unexposed interesting stuff. The chances of someone turning a torch on it are getting smaller and smaller.

Where does the portrait of Philippe Thys hang in the cycling gallery? The triple Tour winner of the Tour the France, from the nevertheless sporty Anderlecht (in Brussel, Belgium), never received a book as a gift for his top performances. Thys was not the most accessible rider of his era. He was even a bit at odds with his time: he was always watching the clock and could resist large pieces of fat bacon and 'french' fries.

Philippe was a great gentleman, who could rule and patronise in the race like Merckx or Hinault. Always in moderation. He did not need to put out superdominance for weeks to be happy himself. Introverted Thys preferred to dress up immediately after a carefully chosen exploit in a stoic cipher genre Anquetil or Indurain. He certainly belongs in that list of lap killers.

The athletic Brussels native won the Tour in 1913, 1914 and 1920. Four crucial years were lost in the Great War, blocking his Tour counter at three. Louison Bobet managed to match that winning streak just three decades later. Thys was a paragon of regularity and plan. He had all the natural qualities a Tour rider needs and was very rarely impulsive or reckless. Yet a perceived obviousness around cobbled-together extra wins requires putting into perspective. The Tour back then had unpredictable nasty edges. Anyone who won the Tour in its pioneering years could easily have lost it in as many as 10 of the 15 stages that same year. Tides could take hours and were daily on the appeal. Wheel, handlebar and fork breaks, gore falls, dubious penalties, barely counterable slumps, tainted evening meals and poisoned drink cans lurked, along every sward of 10,000 kilometres of road verge.

All contenders had an almost equally abondant drawing right to misery. From that odds table emerged a winner, often weaker that year than his direct opponent. That opponent might then win the following year ... when another unbeatable master was outsmarted by that one unevenness in that one patch of fog ... or never again.

Anyone who reads ride reports of the time and milks the gross exaggerations penetrates the universal rules of sport and the pattern of all cycling times; whether the road is in billiard flat asphalt or pointy mountain flint. Reckless phenomena colour the course but usually end up literally and figuratively on the sidelines. Those with no allies and nothing to give away will find it hard to win. Those who are equally good almost every day will sooner or later drive the opposition into failure. It's as simple as that. Thys had understood that wonderfully. After three wins, probability flows unmistakably quietly into statistical mathematics. Even if it seems that Philippe took advantage of his secure insights, caution is still required. Traits of riders are all too often exaggerated and, after crunching comparisons with other generations, puffed up into a sublimating creamy puff. It is therefore better to wield a trembling and doubting pen, just tell the story and only look forward or backward by mouth.

The newsprint of his time didn't much like nor praised the Belgian riding for the french Peugeot team. Never at willin the effort, never spectacular in the slump. Dry and colourless: that must have been the problem. Karel Van Wijnendaele –Belgiums most notorious cycling journalist – was unfairly silent about Thys for a long time and only came to the realisation at a late age, that what he had managed required a lot of class. Tour de France boss Desgrange found him cycling too often between the others' bad luck and the editors of the French-language gazettes from Brussels were still too often on the horse races to do him justice.

Philippe is in bold in all rankings worldwide. Those who want to know more about him are referred to a meagre italicised footnote. Being a Brussels native was not a good idea even in his time. The country's power centre did have prestige, but it was home to mishmash of people, not egged on as a minor ardent or a rooting crofter. There was no shortage of pub landlords giving koerskes in Brussels. Nor were there any sportsmen with white summer mouche who frequented neighbourhood fairs. Young racers on cramped urban garrisons shined up their racing bikes as briskly as their peers elsewhere, dreaming along over the Galibier and soloing to Roubaix. The modern era with its concrete and car parks chased the race out of the capital in no time. No one took any notice immediately. Numerous Brussels legends on and off the bike said goodbye and folded an empty storybook.

Thys himself is said to have once put things on paper and passed them on for review or use. Without consequence. Worse, caught at a time when no copy could be made. If the notes do turn up, parts of this book are ridiculously incomplete. As long as they remain hidden, at least this edition is an attempt to put a face to the muscular stowaway. Philippe is entitled to that anyway. At the end of his cycling career, he put the racing bike in his coach without hesitation and never looked in the rear-view mirror again. A hopeful trail led to his grandson and daughter-in-law. Sweet people who would have loved to help, but had barely heard parrainte stories themselves. The travelling entrepreneurs did not sit at the table together often enough. Pity that son Theo, who knew more, had died far too early. Thys single-handedly took his history in image and object to the Paris Sports Museum. That museum is closed, the packed collection now on its way to a new home in Nice. The three-time winner of the Tour de France has by no means made a piece of work around his person easy. Out of sheer politeness, he would have found the effort to bring him out of oblivion at least very kind of us..

BRUXELLES — Chaussée de Mons

1889

At the Willebroek bridge

A week after the ugly tumble of cyclist Emiel De Beuckelaer - heritage of the famous Elixer d'Anvers alcoholic drink brewers - in the Belgian boneshaker championship, 18-year-old Caroline Van Grimbergen, a true 'Brusselès' (nickname given to women of Brussels), gives birth to Philippe Thys in

Emile de Beuckelaer ▲

Anderlecht. It is the morning of 8 October 1889. The first chocolate trams (after their colour) have been running through Brussels for several years and the Scheut-priests have left en masse for Congo shortly before.

At the beginning of July the same year, the 'cabaretière' (collective name for both manager, musician and foor actress) married Desiré Thys, five years older. Caroline's mother comes from an Anderlecht branch that has kept a pub for gen-erations. Spiteful working-class people, who like to do commerce and accumu-late a lot of people skills. Grandfather is a barrel maker, a handy side job in an innkeeper's family. There are nine children. Mother Marie will become pregnant again at 47, after daughter Line has already given birth to her Philippe.

Did Caroline's flame, Desiré, thirsty happen to walk into the inn by herself? A slip of the road with consequences? Thys sr. is from Willebroek. Or at least, he was born there in 1866 into a bargee family that literally ran down the banks of the canal. They mostly sailed from the Rupel to the Anderlecht Gate and back. Then, sooner or later, they bump into an oncoming ship. This is how Desiré was created, on the move. Not in the darkness of a stifling ship's cabin, later athleticism would show, but under the healthy bare sky. Beside the thistle berm of the waterway. Through the persuasive work of father, born in the Klein-Brabant canal parish of Ruisbroek with a ship's cap. Through the doubtful impotence of mother, skipper girl from the capital, who will and won't and will and won't and finally likes. A seductive siren on the bow? It sounds hardly romantic; but the likelihood that she had to pull the barge along, harnessed as a human horse, is many times more realistic.

The proud skipper moors in Willebroek so that his wife Agnes can give birth to the little one. Their five children are born in four different places, as far away as the Walloon region. Once adolescent, Diseré will step out of his prescribed exist-ence as a water nomad. He wants to learn a stile and live in a real house. It is now his turn to seduce a young 'Zinneke' (proud inhabitant of Brussels).

An allegiance of musts as it is called in the local vernacular is the result. That the conception preceded the rattling off of the gospel and code civil does not sound like anything special in those times. Nor is it dishonourable, although the degree of maternal well-being is taken as a yardstick by the ever-present gossiping aunts at the podes of church and town hall to express, to a greater or lesser extent, vicarious shame.

The same July day, the brand-new couple takes up residence at '115, Chaussée de Mons', in the heart of Cureghem district (in the heart of Brussels). Philippe Thys starts his cycling career belly kicking, the day the Groenendaal horse racing track opens. He will make money from it later, by supplying enough punters. The world's longest green will soon be paradise and hell in one for many. Well and truly three months later, the proud milliner's son breathes in 'Brettanomyces Bruxellensis' and 'Lambicus' for the first time (famous yeasts who give the famous 'Kriek' beers their unique taste and scent). Affluent the family is not exactly. But father Desiré is a self-confident man, a commissioned piece worker who can pass on love for his craft. 'Flup' (a Brussels nickname for 'Philippe') does not come into the world to jaded proles, who wonder after every gin rush what life is actually for. In the summer of 1890, the young family gladly moves to 'Rue Prévinaire', a much quieter neighbourhood by the railway bund and ca-nal. At that spot, Anderlecht is still a tangled amalgam of town and countryside, though its green foliage is definitively tarnished by brick factories and cadaver-ous hangars.

▲ Chaussée de Mons, Anderlecht.

Mother can tell beautiful stories. About what lies beyond the street corner and used to look many times more idyllic. About pale meadows and roads amidst flowery meadows, along which city dwellers promenaded to the three islands in the river Zenne. About the welcoming front doors of whitewashed Anderlecht houses, which then stood exclusively in the extension of the 'Pajottenland' (the rural Brussels hinterland) and deliberately turned their backs on the city. Mother Thys still hung around in the meadows, on the banks of the Zenne branches and along the paths of the 'Pedebeek'.

This gurgled into the river at the old croft of The Island, where shorn maids used to throw carreaux of ammunition over long tables in summer in the courtyard of the doening, two by two. It was summer ritual, in the crisp cloudless early hours of what would soon become a heated Sunday and before the steppe and coquette mademoiselles arrived. At the mills of the Middelzenne and the Bollickx wolf farm (where the Brussels Zenne still runs above ground today), taking stock of the amount of geuven and goujons being caught was a classic city outing. In the taverns along the waterway, the fish has been on the menu for years: as a fried snack similar to bouchterink or cold à l'escabeche. At the Thys home, one is not inclined to eat that half-contaminated food of only head and bones anymore. The carefully brushed canvas full of rural delight has been brutally nicked and snatched away by excavations for the widening of the ABC axis (Antwerp-Brussels-Charleroi). The widened canal forms a nasty barrier and a traffic jam Indiennne of cotton farms soon surrounds the dark and morose wound for several kilometres.Gais comme un canal: Brel will later sing. The Dam on the other side and the Broekbeek valley, nourisher of the ponds of d'Aumale, is given up and parceled out. The Quartier Birmingham and Cureghem become important municipal neighbourhoods. Further down Molenbeek begins Little Manchester, an intense industrial tangle reminiscent of the British industrial city. Across the canal bridges, for the original population, the city begins. In Thys's toddler years, 30,000 people already live on that canal side. With his first steps, the little one already gets attention for physical leisure activities. This is quite exceptional for that time. Sport is still in its infancy.

People, after a long day's work and weeding a small vegetable garden, are many times too tired to fill their last stonde with effort. Most have a chronic lack of disposition and barely manage to complete the most necessary things. Cycling is trendy and very expensive: the privilege of affluent citizens. Young dandies, charming idlers and future lawyers with rich daddies set up cycling clubs.

Jointly enjoying Sunday outings, picnics and paper hunts are the typical club activities. At last, man can move independently via mecanique and chart a course of his own. Tyre repair remains precarious and a blot on the immense joy of movement.

The elite cycling clubs are network gatherings, new replacement environments for work-related confrontations. Leisure is born: Sundays completely detached from work or religious pressures. Cycling is summer fun. Winter months adorn le président d'honneur, qui doit savoir donner, in dull and better speeches. Speeches are followed by soupers, musical evenings and stage performances.

For many, the physical exertion can never straighten out what frequent toasting obligations with gobs of beer and sweet wine, alongside giant portions of red meat and generous capons, do. The fat edge of cycling mania is more than considerable and many a notorious club member is laid to rest at an early age, regretfully succumbing to blood drive or colics.

This is not the world of father Thys, who will not have a bicycle for a long time. A second-hand one costs about 150 francs or four months' wages. A wage earner cannot save that amount of money. However, Desiré would have been only too happy to try the velo. He was an excellent gymnast, who in his younger years competed in running races and could regularly win. Genetically, for borling Philippe, things were already in order there.

▲ Barges docked in Ruisbroek, on the Brussels-Willebroek Canal.

▲ Vader Désiré Thys   ▲ Cureghem, Anderlecht.

1re Année. — N° 162   10 CENTIMES   Dimanche 15 Juillet 1903

L'ACTUALITÉ

FRANÇAISE, ÉTRANGÈRE, ARTISTIQUE & LITTÉRAIRE ILLUSTRÉE

REVUE DE LA FAMILLE

Pasquin   Aucouturier   Garin   Fischer

LE TOUR DE FRANCE. — Le départ à Villeneuve-Saint-Georges

1894

The Cureghem slaughterhouses

The place where a person is born is never neutral for the course of life. In the rigid countryside, village notables roar against anyone who wants to go faster than horse and cart. There are bans on modernity instituted, on anything that does not resemble work or church attendance. Many a sporting talent there remains snubbed in ambitions until after WWI, obliged under peer pressure to put away dreams. In that respect, rue Prévinaire is a better habitat.

Coureageous Flup takes his first fast steps and grows up on fresh milk from the Sheep Carré, which is wheeled out daily 'me 't'onekeir' (with a dog cart). The popular neighbourhood is full of entrepreneurial spirit. Those who know their way around don't have to traipse on the spot. Cureghem is a district in change, where the 'Société anonyme des Abattoirs et Marchés d'Anderlecht-Cureghem' is opening a grand building. Such an imposing glass canopy has rarely been seen. It requires di-version of the Zenne arm and a foundation almost five metres deep: the later cellars. Otherwise, Anderlecht's cast-iron pride would certainly sink into the boggy canal brooks. The canal to Charleroi on one side and the Rupel in the other, took over the job of the dirty city river.

The new waterway is not the wide green-silver ribbon that later necessitated the construction of the immensely long Pont Van Praet. The navigation is still tailor-made for the bakeekes: a specially built barge coupled in series to a tug, just fitted through all the locks. The little boats ferry coal from the Borinage mining pits and bricks from Boom. Between Anderlecht and Molenbeek, an area

of coal sellers, brewers, metalworkers and, near the abattoirs, tanners and food manufacturers is brewing.

The zone is fast becoming a steaming mess, providing a lot of work and thus making everyone better, most of all the entrepreneurs themselves. On the south-west side of la ville grows a vranke and free zone where the street belongs to everyone. That large hordes of workers occupy it from time to time feels no more palatable to the bourgeoisie of the time than the Balkan used-car business that now dwells there.

For four years, Flupke may continue to claim all family concerns. The absence of more offspring at the Thys home was exceptional for the time, but private: miscar-riages, infant mortality and sexual complications were painfully common. At the end of February 1893, Flup finally has a sister. Josephine-Louise is a beautiful girl, who will assist him considerably when she also turns up in Paris in wartime. Sister marries her fugitive Brussels taximan in the distant city of lights in 1917 and a year later they have a son, Philippe ... Could the adoration for her then already famous brother be any greater? Sweet Louise dies at just 29. Of this impending sadness, the family fortunately has no knowledge yet.

In the late spring of 1894, a good 15 months after the little sister, brother Michel is already there. Thysje's little brother is une copie de l'aîné. He will try to follow the eldest on a bicycle, before becoming a bacon butcher. Anyone who wants to know his exploits should look for Guillaume Thys. Naming is a strange and com-plicated phenomenon in many families. Why grandfather Michel's name is sud-denly renounced in custom and replaced by that of uncle,is one such bizarre case. One should not necessarily look for family squabbles behind it. An identical name descendant through another line, often sufficed, to suddenly call Lowie under the domestic low ceiling conveniently our French.

There are plans for a new cycling track, now that the one on the Germanystraat (now Clemenceaulaan) has fallen into disuse. The Veloce Club Cureghem-Anderlecht is the young ambitious cycling club that pushes the cart vigorously with only 22 mem-bers. It can count on some solid racing cyclists: Rasseneur, Van Wichelen, Jonas and Freudenthal. The Anderlecht mayor Moreau accepts the honorary presidency at the club premises, '47, Boulevard d'Anderlecht'. He knows only too well that this will entail the commitment for a building permit. It must move forward.

The new runway was ready by spring 1895, because its management board includes such names as Solvay and Colruyt, figures who are counted among the economic youngsters of Brussels. The Bruxelles-Midi axle track measures exactly 804.5 me-tres, is eight metres wide and opens on Easter Sunday. On the programme is an unu-sual long-distance number: the six-hour course. Lesna wins and clocks off at 17.20 at 202.613 kilometres or almost 34 average. That is faster than the first automobile that tumbles through Brussels shortly afterwards.

Philippe is now almost a metre tall. Could it be, that he is somewhere between the bars of the wooden fence watching? Perhaps sub-tly sent away from home with an excuse, where they find their second breath? Once again, the Thys family expands consider-ably, with three daughters: Jeanne, Marie and, in 1903, the offspring Dorothée-Elis-abeth.

She descends into the cervix as the final piece of the family tree, at the very mo-ment when one Abran at the 'Au Réveil Matin' inn lowers his flag. A special cycle race takes off on the southern edge of Paris: the very first Tour de France.

▲ The leader pack, with Brange and Garin in the lead, in the first Tour de France, 1903.

This is a silly stunt by the editor-in-chief of the daily news- and sportspaper L'Auto, a trou-bled company hoping to boost its circulation figures. The adventurers soon set off into the Forêt de Sénart - at the time, together with the forests of Fontainbleau and Vincennes, one big forest that extended to the outskirts of the city - towards Melun. Cycling was virtually extinct in the Belgian capital at the time. Only a handful of pioneers still occasionally turn laps on the track of the Bois de la Cambre. The last Thys descendant finally sees the light of day, when Garin has already won the very first tour stage and, against a warm wall in Lyon, carelessly lights yet another self-rolled cigarette.

When Elisabeth is snoozing in her cot, sprightly Flup ialready preparing to jump out of school, into real life. Thys competes in foot races. Like father like son. La foulle along the road, whips up the street boys as they start the sprint towards a better pair of slippers, sweets or a nice basket of fruit. Medically Responsible Sports Practice is not watching those days. The running races are the sporting measure of the poor. Desiré's son is strong and alert, becomes fascinated by technology and feeds his eyes everywhere. Curiosity drives everything. Philippe is quick of mind and limb and becomes a commissioner at the House of Phonographers. Young guys, who car-ry parcels and do all sorts of jobs, then get to work in seething Brussels without any problems. Time is not yet an issue and speed is not even for sale. In 1904, the then provincial government of Brabant counted 663 automobiles and 691 motocyclettes on its territory. A few dozen owners in Leuven, Tienen, Vilvoorde and a handful of modernist estate barons notwithstanding, all these hopping, crashing rigs were cruising around Brussels. They do not yet pose a threat to cycling life, when Thys first takes the start of a velocross race in his own town in 1907. In the meantime, he had been hired as a domestique (domestic servant) by a wealthy family.

The steward has loaned bright Philippe the only ladies' bicycle in the house after much nagging. The Anderlecht pumpers are on a family trip to Namur that day. During a boat trip, the steamer hits a bridge and the iron frame of the roof canvas collapses. Two broken shoulders, a shattered hand and more broken ribs have to be taken to hospital. Flupke, meanwhile, takes his chance in a home race. The cycling debut is not a success, but the young Brusseler does not give up and soon contests more district races. Over a good 20 or 25 kilometres, weekly active riders compete in them against occasional actors of all ages and sizes. The term popular entertain-ment covers the load better than cycling.

▲ Maurice Garin, the first Tour winner.

▲ Poithier, Garin and Augerau, the first three of the 1903 Tour de France, enjoy a cup of champagne.

▲ The Bois de la Cambre cycling track.

NOËL-VÉLO

ÉDITÉ PAR LE JOURNAL "LE VÉLO"

1908

1908

The Queen of the seaside towns

Fragile Philippe is flagged off third somewhere and that does not escape an eager little industrious person. Thys is lucky. Soon a Saphir racing bike with regular tyres is waiting for him. The benefactor is cycling mad and has a small factory at the Midi, where excellent material is made. The branch plate for the bike still costs just six francs in Brabant instead of ten. That amount will not stop Thyske.

He joins the 'Union Cycliste Anderlechtois' as a real racing driver. UCA is yet another sporting initiative in the district. After another interlude, choosing Anderlecht Sportif as its name, it is finally Cureghem Sportif, which will bring cycling stability to the commune in 1911. Thys will curiously never become a member there, brother Guillaume will. After a complete slump around the turn of the century, solid amateur clubs such as 'Sporting Club de Bruxelles', 'Linthout Velo', 'Laken Sportif' and 'Brussel Sportif' reappear. These give road races more attention.

The brand-new clubs represent pure amateur sport with standing. They attract riders who do it for cups and medals, at most reaching out for in-kind prizes. It is a new story, far removed from the magouille (evil scheming) in the bestial street races, laced with cheating and drunkenness. By the time new club leaders and their feted athletes want to make a point; it is already glaringly obvious to Philippe that the shadowy fairground rides are not his thing. In 1908, he takes an LVB union licence and takes his chances with the amateur category.

In Brussels Sportif's season opener on Easter Monday, he could actually follow Guillaume Coeckelberg as a pair of shorts. At the time, Coeckelberg was the domi-nant cycling crack - there were hardly any pros - among the amateurs. Over a carpet of snow, they plod through Walloon Brabant together in the GP Vincart and climb the dreaded Mont Saint Paul. The tourist riders, who were allowed to start 21 min-utes earlier, have to step aside for the leading duo. The finish is on the track in the Bois de la Cambre. Thys arrives there four min-utes after his renowned breakaway companion: a particularly handsome debut. The following Sunday, he is third in the GP Alcyon, half a wheel after De Blauwe. Coeckelberg wins solo again. He ran the two obligatory laps around the track, due to a late puncture. The winner spent five hours on the road for about 100 kilometres.

The Karreveld-velodrome will open in May - the foundation stone will not be laid until 22 March. Liege-Brussels will get the scoop. But most ride the wrong way along the way and Aloïs Verstraeten, who turns up the track as primus, is later relegated to second place. Philippe is not in fine form that day and reaches the Koekelberg hill with difficulty. From there, it's head in cash free-wheels to the ponds of Molenbeek.

On 21 June, Thys is fit again and travels to faraway Hasselt, to colour the start of cycling in Limburg and the Kempen region. The peloton struggles to get going: the Holy Procession is ahead and the pavement is full of people. Together with Alfons Lauwers from Wezemaal, he decides the race. The final chord must be set on the Kuringersteenweg. The street name evokes a

▲ Riders at the start of the Grand Prix Alcyon.

▲ The peloton in Hoegaarden, with Thys and Coussement in the lead

▶ Coeckelbergh and Thys while climbing Mont St. Paul and Jolibois.

▲ Riders at the start of the Grand Prix Vincart.

▲ In 1908, Philippe Thys finishes second in the Grand Prix Vincart, on his Saphir cycling bike. Guiilaume Coeckelbergh is the winner of this race.

1. Beckx de Hasselt, premier des Limbourgeois au moment où M. Keyenberg, que l'on voit à droite, vient de lui remettre une palme. — 2. Sur la route. De Brée à Beverloo. Le peloton de tête vu de dos. — Entre Saint-Trond et Tongres. Le peloton de tête. Roland de Soignies mène Coeckelberg en seconde position. Verstraeten en troisième position. — 4. Lauwers de Louvain, le vainqueur du Tour du Limbourg. — 5. A Hechtel. Le peloton de tête est arrêté par le passage à niveau. — 6. Vue prise après la course, au banquet offert par M. Keyenberg. — 7. Thys de Bruxelles, arrivé second à Hasselt. — 8. L'automobile du Vélo. La Meuse du garage d'Hooge. Devant se trouve M. Keyenberg, l'organisateur du Tour du Limbourg. Sur le marche-pieds, notre Directeur A. Collignon. Dans la voiture MM. Posenaer et Bupsse et M. Quadvlieg, professeur à l'Athenée de Hasselt, correspondant du Vélo pour le Limbourg. — 9. Lucien Kranskens, le benjamin de la course, arrivé 6e. — 10. En Campine. Entre Tongres et Brée, le peloton de tête vu de dos. — 11. A Hasselt. Vue prise avant le départ. — 12. A trois kilomètres de Saint-Trond, le peloton de tête vu de dos. — Au numéro 2 on remarque l'auto du Vélo.

sense of home. Flup believes in it, but less than a kilometre from the banner on the Brussels Grand-Place (the amazing central square of the City of Brussels), stupidly slides out, over oxtail poop. Damn.

The sharpness is back. Time to prove something. Flup decides to duel with the Floorers. A fourth place in the 'Ronde der Vlaanders' – the Tour of Flanders for enthusiasts (non-professionals) is already very hopeful. Strong Vandenberghe gets the lion ribbon. In the village race of Jette, another win falls just short. Then comes the event of the year: the Tour of Belgium. The stage race for amateurs enjoyed great success in 1907 thanks to the participation of French stars such as Lapize, Cruchon and Trousselier.

In multi-day racing, Thys has no experience whatsoever. He will be given improved equipment for the round. That should help him progress a few kilometres faster anyway. From home, there is a lot of sympathy and support, but little money. Fortunately, the city has well-farming merchants and small entrepreneurs of ordinary origin. Their dream soon comes true: they work their way up to become respectable citizens. Above the sneaky grandeur of the distinguished salons, where they will never really belong, they prefer the sympathy of the street and the people. They want to make the papers and the photo and become the acclaimed kings of their neighbourhood or commune. That is why they put money into sports and club life. Everything Flup manages to scrounge up in support comes from that patronage. So he and 108 others can stand on the Brouckère square poppelling. He checks his light tubes again. The new rubber will have to assist him for 146 kilometres to Moorslede. The village of arrival is the home of Cyrille Van Hauwaert, the best Belgian rider and already a legend after victories in Bordeaux-Paris (1907), Milan-Sanremo and Paris-Roubaix (1908).

The learning curve is harder than expected. There is considerable time loss in the first stage, and approaching the finishing line in the second stage to Ostend, the police cannot control the crowd. Trousselier drives into a spectator. There is a banal cart in the road and on the other side, wrought-iron park lights. The city by the sea has undergone a metamorphosis in a few decades. Courtesy of Leopold II, who had a fancy residence built there and carried numerous noble copycats in his wake. The ugly fishwife finds a whirlwind way out along chic avenues and promenades, cloaks herself in bluestone and becomes Queen. Against her abandoned bumper

◀ Report of the Tour de Limburg of amateurs. In frame number 7:
"Philippe Thys from Brussels is second in the stage to Hasselt".

– 25 –

cart with dried flatfish and crumpets collides a Brussels man. Unfortunate Thys is immediately taken away with a gushing head wound. After a brief hospital stay, for him the race can begin again.

The Belgian round has arrived by then. Lauwers wins on points, although the moral victory is again for Guillaume Coeckelberg. He hijacks all but two of the stages. During one unlucky day, he loses all prospects of overall victory. The seaside accident has triggered something in Thys. He is more awake than ever before. The organizers of Marchienne-Mons-Marchienne will write him on their list of honours. At Remouchamps a short time later, he will again receive gladioli and cups.

Together with Julot, there are wins in a 75-kilometre team race and the small medal at the Championship of Europe tandem race. During a Belgium-France in late September, the Karreveld track is so slippery that the mob crashes ingloriously during the first circumference.

Philippe refuses to take the restart. In the audience, four-year-old Marcel Boogmans from Koekelberg sits looking admiringly at the riders and their clean velomachines. During the reveillon (New Year's Eve) of 1926, he and Thys will still ride the Brussels Six-Day race. Capital cycling advances, despite the slippery surface. After Karreveld, the beautiful 265-metre track of Linthout Velo is under construction on Tervurenlaan in Woluwe. Sport while also fighting its way into the newspaper columns.

▲ René Vandenberghe   ▲ Jules Coussement   ▲ Paul Deman

In December, the cycling scene moves to the smoky back room of inn Het Gulden Kasteel on Boulevard d'Anderlecht. The racers pedal on the spot in winter, on exercise bikes. They are daunting devices that rattle like the mechanism of a church clock, driven by chains. Technology no longer stands still. Large pints of Faro and Export are tapped while youngsters sprint on the rollers. Thys will be up against De Blauwe and Verstraete.

▲   Deulens and Jules Patou competing in the Prix du Printemps cyclo-cross organized by Bruxelles-Sportif.

1908 has barely ticked away when at the famous Four Arms crossroads, the wind pierces through marrow. It is very early. The first Frisian Elfstedentocht has been secretly run. What lies ahead in the Brussels forest is of the same idiosyncratic calibre. A stocky figure in jockey jersey from UCA rides warm-up rides and attracts the attention of a group of connoisseurs trampling the cold. Before the year end, in a similar trial through muddy no-man's land, that striped lad has clobbered Salès, the former national champion and pro rider. Whoever wants to follow him will have to have good legs.

No one succeeds in that. Philippe Thys is by far the best of 47 starters in the very first major cyclo-cross race. This cycling branch is no more than a training session on the road bike then. Obstacles and mud are not sought in cross-country running either. The road season is much more important than the playful madness that comes over from France.

Despite superb fitness, there are no sea flowers waiting for Flup anywhere. In Antwerp-Menen, Jules Coussement from Rumbeke is half a wheel faster. His only major victory earns him only a small footnote in cycling history. Thys is fat with it. Brussels-Menen goes fine until Paul Deman - the first winner of the Tour of Flanders four years later - steps in. After a second place at the Prize of Tubize, a bonkers cobblestone from Laken perforates his pneu in the Championship of cycling brand WKC. What misery. In Torhout, things finally work out and Philippe wins the six-hour race against everything the province can muster in terms of strong devils.

When Charel Verbist crashes on the velodrome of 't Karreveld on 21 July, he is the next death in a long line of daredevils. The daredevils go many times too fast for their unreliable petrol engines. The riders are pulled along in their wake to insane speeds above 100 kilometres per hour. A few months before, fiddling with engines and petrol was already costing cycling-loving Ypres and its newly opened velodrome dearly. The moment the third stage of the Tour of Belgium was due to arrive, the wings were on fire. The dry velodrome wood is the next inferno and the participants in the national round are forced to abandon their ride.

In late July, Flup finally cycles off all despair in the Tour de Braband. Blériot was the first to fly a plane across the canal the previous day, a milestone. The first powered flight took place barely six years earlier. Fly away. They have not yet left Cinquantenaire Park or Thys is already shaking off Aerts and Bruggeman in Tervuren. For hours he gives his all. Lonely and alone. At the Karreveld, he is allowed to go straight onto the grass, as the track once again shines like a mirror. Then it's 31 boring minutes of waiting until Molenbeek home rider Heyvaert shows up. Flup has finally grabbed a big prize.

In the tail end of the course, a few collided with a motor vehicle and that is talking stuff. Traffic conflicts are far from being a problem, but the mishmash of cars and motorbikes, bikes, horse-drawn carts and drovers is quietly demanding order and rules. After compulsory right-hand driving across the country, fuss follows already. Cars will henceforth have to carry two instead of just a single white light and turn it on shortly after sunset. Motorised vehicles get the privilege of a horn. Bicycles are allowed to have a bell and must turn on lights an hour after sunset. What a complicated state of affairs.

Philippe's carburettor bulb is fine and the condition should be more than adequate for a puking Tour of Belgium. It's quite disappointing. After a mediocre 12th place in the opening stage to Menen, bad luck strikes again near Ostend. Those who reach Bruges in 26th place know that a good final result can be forgotten on points. Follow uselessly to Leuven? Towards Verviers wasting forces? Flup is no longer in the mood.

▲ The Le Collier des Saphirs team participating in the 1908 Tour de Belgium. From left to right: Philippe Thys; Roland, Cassiers, Toussain, Thuriot, Remy, Van Meerhaegen, Bettens, Gillard, team masseur Alb.Wilmus, sports director Marcel, L. Vincart, constructor of the Saphir bicycles, Valloton, Huart, Baudelet, and Everaerts.

▲ Coeckelbergh and Everaerts behind the contest's grand prize: a motorcycle donated by La Dernière Heure newspaper.

▲ Lauwers, winner of the Tour de Limburg and the Tour de Belgium

It's not right in the cup. Something is. A tricky subject has not let the hairy twenty-something go all summer. He was forced to register in the municipal militia register a year before: awaiting the awful draw. A placeke as an auxiliary agent to the municipality neatly circumvented a possible soldierhood proactively, but would the conscrits system be abolished any time soon? There was talk of general conscription for the eldest son of each family. Things could move fast and it would be brutal bad luck.

▲ Ypres velo dream goes up in flames

When the Belgian round finally reaches the capital on 17 August, Thys and fellow townsman Milleke Aerts - later a member of Karel Van Wijnendaele's Flandriens - are already in the piste test of the preliminary programme. He may have to recharge at the start of October for Sedan-Brussels. The final race is in a minor mood, as clammy and grey Paris-Tours sometimes evokes. October races often need no more shortly after the exit: because they no longer exude an ounce of enthusiasm. The furnishing weekly Nos Sports is experiencing the worst day in its short-lived history. It is pouring water and finally only a brave handful of athletes navigate into the - again - flooded oval at the Molenbeek deep end. Thys perseveres and is sixth on the soaked results sheet.

Leopold II did not have long to go after a fierce and clean life. He has given Belgium a colony, alongside so many beautiful avenues and imposing buildings. Will he lure Thys with the last ink from his porte plume? The king waits until 1 December 1909. Only on his deathbed does he sign the law on military service, and the government, lacking beds and equipment, will delay for years before introducing it. Philippe can remain a racing driver and a wout (Brussels swear word for constable).

PHILIPPE THYS
Le Champion d'Anderlecht

1910

At the Pajols

On a misty February evening, Thys pulls up a chair at the Pajols' banquet at Taverne Alfred, rue du Midi (now a 'Pepe Jeans'-shop). The visit is not accidental. Flup opted for the club of Brabant federation president Hubert Baudot. The white club, with its pomegranate-coloured jersey vest, is fast becoming the most prestigious capital city cycling club. In the beautiful Brasserie Flamande on Ortsstraat, notables avec gibus (high flapping hat) gather weekly, who get to sit around the board table with progenitor Delhaize.

Membership of Brussels Sportif is hype. Many capital city tastemakers stride day and night after the grandeur of Paris and Vienna. They adore bleached vegetables, blanquette de veau and fragrant viennoiseries. They revel in the culture of body culture and hygiene, transformed into sporting fraternité by chunky club structures from both exemplary metropolises.

Brussels has to constantly catch up in all areas to stay à jour. So another Exposition Universelle is in the pipeline. The jet set is looking for a site near Solbosch, on the border of the receding forest. The commune of Ixelles has to cave in. Brussels capital finally retains a hefty 62-hectare area extension and builds a new district in exchange. It is also transforming Mont des Arts (now partly the Albertina) into a green corniche. A playful level change of up to 50 metres is waiting for architect Vacherot.

Where the squalid St Rochus district lets its idle poverty roll into town, comes a wide staircase of fountains, waterfalls and sculptures. Magnificent. Never seen! It can't be beat. At the turn of Tervuren, the Colonial Palace (later Africa Museum) opens. The Palace and Astoria hotels, with hundreds of luxury rooms serving the many foreign visitors, are on the rise. However, the term world fair is relative. Participation is limited, but 20 flying flags are enough to convince the masses.

Afterwards, the Compagnie d'Exposition may only register a net profit of 100,000 francs. Without misfortune, it could have been much more. Local entrepreneurs will take advantage. If not with the construction of temporary palaces and praalbows, at least via the supply of fine foodstuffs, the sale of fancy hats, millions of tasty waffles and the complete flow of puffy breweries.

Money attracts money and makes new money. Some have so much of it, they don't know what to do with it. Thys's clearheadedness knows how the world on display works. Looking for facilities himself is no longer necessary. He is right in the middle of the fine fleur of cycling fathers with money and connections. These are happy to give advances on the benefits of the lucrative world exhibition that will follow. Eighty members take their seats behind starched table linen. Flup receives an offer from Walloon bike manufacturer and cycling mecenas Depas to spend a few months in Andenne. There he can complete thorough training in the foothills of the Ardennes. Monsieur Depas is about to open a modern bicycle factory in Seilles and attracts the cream of Walloon cycling at the time: Linart, Marchand, Salmon, Heusghem and Sellier. Father and son Thys do not hesitate for a second. Desiré supports Flup to the

▲ Victor Linart   ▲ Félix Sellier   ▲ Hector Hesughem

hilt. 1910 should be the year of the breakthrough. The national cyclo-cross champi-onship, an open title race across the Sonian forest, is his first target.

Jacques Vanopendebosch, co-founder of Brussel Sportif and father of Cross-country, sees his brainchild finally getting attention. Many are only now discover-ing the cross. Philippe has been ahead of them and, as a former runner, stays one step ahead of everyone. In the road races, things are less smooth. Delays and wheel breakage in a drizzling Antwerp-Meulebeke, squeeze his sickly throat. Spring is plugging away.

Mindful of the permanent dog weather, Devil Olieslagers and sprinter Van Den Born have put the bike aside for good. They are discovering something new, many times more punishing. In the Nice flyweight race, they are on course for a win and in between in the spring sunshine.

Thys also wants to see the azure Central Sea one day. For now, he continues to toil through cloudy homeland. In the smog of Charleroi-Namen-Charleroi, he has to underperform Cooman, but on 31 May, the Brussels rider will shake off the strong Valckenaers in the Circuit des Ardennes. Flup will ride solo to Liège. Poor organisa-tion and fraud along the way, get a tailspin. The cycling federation cancels the result. Meanwhile, in Anderlecht, they have discovered a new crack. Géne Symons pushes

▲ Van Den Born   ▲ Jan Olieslagers, 'the antwerp devil'

his bicycle third over the gruelling chalk line of the Course du Premier Pas, a talent show for youngsters copied from France. The course quickly gained national renomeé. Victim of its own success, more and more entrants show up every year: sometimes as many as 400. When the head of the course dives into Wemmel, the tail is still lining up at Bockstael.

The first cherries make Thys happier than his results. Along at the front during the Tour of Limburg, he does not even make it to sprints, tired and exhausted. In Luxembourg-Brussels, the force is lacking and Salmon wins. Philippe ranks only fourth among the Depas disciples. Mediocrity bothers him. In the national championship at Ransart, he is again among the first overturners of the day and has to chase heavily. It goes fast and the distance is too short to recover and appear at the front. Early July may finally take a tentative step towards resurgence. In Mouscron-Ghent and back, Nordist Vandaele reigns supreme. Thys gets to the lowest podium. On his exceptional aptitude and regularity, everyone agrees. Yet he rides the year around behind.

There is a lot of bad luck involved, but that cannot explain everything. The move to Depas' half-factory team was supposed to provide a significant leap forward, but Philippe is sauntering to the top instead of setting powerful examples. There is nothing left to do but to make the Tour of Belgium a main target once more, even though it has always failed in the past. In the stage through the Ardennes, Thys strikes near Chimay. He gains up to three minutes, but then his pace weakens and he pukes everything out of his body. Weakened, sick and exhausted, the classification is lost yet again. In Verviers, he clocks another ten full minutes loss on Mottiat. Then the motility is gone.

In Leuven, they stormed to the finish with 24 and Thys did not relinquish the lead. No one should finish near him. Drawing up the results takes time. Because the round is contested on points, the exact ranking is important. The judges have no footage or photographic equipment at their disposal yet, but are making a mess of things nonetheless. Teams Colibri and Depas file complaints. They are brutally sent off and subsequently withdraw their riders. The race leaves for Ghent without stage winner Philippe.

During the night of 14-15 August, the people of Brussels did not believe their eyes. Coincidentally asleep in his parents' house after his forced return from Leuven that Sunday night, Flup looks through the skylight. A veritable conflagration blows across the city. What is that? It looks like the historical evocation of the bombing of the Villeroy high on Begelweg, or the repetition of the fire at the Ducal Castle. Imprudent people they are, those merry Brusseleirs.

In 1731, they make jam and think they can casually let the fire smoulder. An hour later, on Coudenberg, Europe's largest palace is on fire. There is no question of putting out the fire on the steep site. It is freezing and then water is not very willing to carry out liquid orders. Innocent suckers among the staff will have to keep up that story to their deaths. The real stokebrand is the governess herself, who falls asleep among the lit candles. Once awakened, according to etiquette, she cannot allow anyone into her private room. One waits too long to break down the door and Lucifer gets free rein.

Today, the next Grand Palais is in the glow, that of the World Expo. Right on the eve of a public holiday and under the eye of many foreign tourists. Even here and now, decent firefighting is no go. Is an over-active cigarette butt from a late lit cigar, which had finaly lost its flavour, the culprit? There goes the profit. Bruxelles Kermesse and the exhibition end in a minor way. From formidable to fort minable.

Next year, Philippe will become independent. In this new series, talented youngsters with pro ambitions will ride a separate competition with cash prizes. There will be rules for constructors who want to set up a team. Thys has already got a taste of the atmosphere in a factory team through Depas. It is the experiences of cycling bosses in allowing controlled material support in the amateur ranks that give rise to the creation of the independents. This temporarily removes the great hypocrisy surrounding pure amateur racing.

The number of amateurs has grown large, but the distance among free riders (pros) scares off many youngsters. The independents are exactly what is needed to give hesitant talent momentum and allow the gap to be bridged. The league will often still redraw series - often too late - under pressure from economic or sociological developments in commerce and society.

Philippe Thijs

1911

Passage Passerieu

T hysThys is somewhere on the road between home and his Ardennes training ground, when the well-known French pro Passerieu suddenly comes riding alongside him. With his London roots, the Frenchman is the world citizen of the peloton. He samples Flupke and challenges him to a playful raid uphill near Wavre. The pro fails to win from the little one.

▲ Georges Passerieu

Thys is waiting for him beyond the summit. The reward is extraordinary. With his first available breath, Passerieu asks the little giant to come to France. By intercession, he can join the renowned Paris Veloclub of Levallois, where talents like Guénot and Valloton are in training. Philippe does not think for long. By constantly coming up against the same riders on the local circuit, progression stalled.

The Belgian cycling world cannot compete with France, where highly developed amateur clubs operate with permanent training masters and have excellent equipment, gymnasiums and sleeping accommodation. Well-known bicycle factories invest heavily in professional teams. Their managers skim amateur matches in between, looking for employable talent.

Levallois - with its many bicycle factories - has a real sporting tradition. It is the playground of the athletic Parisien. Tour winner Trousselier was born in the limbo of the Parisian tub and made cycling a folie général there. The moment Thys gets the offer to join VCL, ex-pistier Paul Ruinart arrives at the head of the white-blacks. He introduces training camps in the south, dietetics, individual training schedules and specific training methods for pistards. All the great French cycling names of the interwar period will pass through his hands. The Passerieu passage takes place in late spring and gives Thys' intentions a different twist after all. Beginning in

March, he cannot even knock on Mother Lambic's establishment in the Bois de la Cambre to defend his cyclo cross title The Belgian championship goes on hold for a year. The otherwise quiet Brussels rider, is reeling. Why shouldn't he take a pro licence? Those who ride around with those independents stick around unnecessarily and only earn half the pennies for almost as long of racing. In any case, he is already getting himself registered for the pro race in Belgium in May and will be sent number 15 under cover.

▲ 'Chez Mother Lambic' in the Bois de la Cambre. Registration site for the cross-country championships.

Family and friends stand to wave him off at the Wheel of Anderlecht for the opening race of the independents. Binche is the finishing point. That Thys will soon beat Passerieu uphill? What fool dreamt that? It takes getting used to the indé's: arriving eighth at the gilles of Binche is not carnivalesque, but neither is it a sparkling debut. Brussels-Liège is another lesson in humility. Most of his competitors are a pack older and that will be the deciding factor in the final. During Antwerpen-Menen things go badly wrong in the Waasland region. Thys has to get off at the kontrool in Ghent with a sprained shoulder. It sounds worse than it is.

Hannut, a sprawling farming village where the Haspengouw countryside comes to buy a shiny shovel and new shoes once every few years, is where the gates of success finally open. Philippe wins a 100-kilometre race there in mid-May, refuels confidence and just a few days later accidentally meets a friend for life. Through his intercession, he is allowed to start in all major French races.

A further coincidence is that the great Peugeot, in family deliberations in Valentigney, makes an extraordinary decision. Bike and car company merge again. Five Peugeot scions join hands. New company policies immediately follow. They suddenly deviate from the outlined path at the mobility giant.

Done one spend masses of resounding francs on the insatiable money hunger of the mini coronet of champions pourri. Peugeot, however, had some great cycling moments in the Tour de France. In 1908, they took all the stages with Petit-Breton Faber, Passerieu, Georget, Cornet, Aucouturier, Dortignac, Garrigou and Paulmier. They row into the top four and places six and eight.

With immediate effect, the bickering with major Parisian rivals stops. The professional factory team is disbanded. Peugeot comes to realise that there are hundreds of talented young riders active in the country, who never get the chance to race beyond the border of their canton. Parisian centralism is already too much of an imprint and this is not helping the broadening of cycling. Efforts will be made from now on to set up youth races for independents. These can earn money and magnifique prizes.

▲ Riders arrive at a checkpoint in the 1910 Tour de France....

Peugeot will support the best youngsters. When they detect real talent in a new generation, they will again consider a team at the top. The selections for the main Peugeot-Wolber criterium races are via a multitude of Championnats Départementaux. Those who can make their mark there will be fished out. The win in Hannut is barely applauded when Thys spurs to Paris for his first foreign appearance. The baptism of fire follows on 25 May: Paris-Robaais for indépendants in one day.

Until Beauvais - a dumbed-down textile town where General Foch will later decide on the Allied settlement of the Great War - Philippe is nicely in the front. Who are the riders he has to guard? Names and back numbers they did give him, but with names come jerseys and faces. Constantly guarding the right men amidst dust and tumult is an impossible task for the newcomer. Pichon and Guénot escape. In Lens, the race is done. Flup finishes seventh, in a chasing group. He certainly does not disappoint.

Sometimes the race provokes not a shred of emotion and the strongest wins over predictable competitors, who are simply left behind somewhere. That is exactly how it went that afternoon towards Roubaix. Flup wins Paris-Toulouse in two

▲ Winner René Guenot at arrival of Paris-Roubaix for Inépendants 1911.

stages just weeks later. Figuet is flat at the back in the final kilometres of the two-stage race. Now there is drama involved. Thys does not miss the opportunity. He shows fond qualities, can wonderfully contain youthful hubris, is tactically mature and is in the lead when it really matters. A lot of young riders go undaunted and are described as exceptional power men in the prologue of newspaper reports. A few chapters later, bulging with cramp, they are deleted from the account.

From the ville rouge (Toulouse is built in red bricks), proud winner Philippe immediately heads home. In the very first Belgian championship for independents, he wants to aim high right away. The course around Bastogne should suit him.

The sizeable leading group stays together as the race is only over 100 kilometres. The calibrated task at a title race still dates back to primal cycling, where time over a set distance was important. The federation does not want to throw that angle overboard. As a result, the race is insufficiently selective and in the sprint fast

▲ Odiel Defraye

Armand Lenoir makes his point. Thys is not even ranked. An hour earlier, another outsider, Odiel Defraeye, took the tricolour among the pros.

Thys remains in the country for a short while to win a criterium in Bertrix and then another, in Huy, to please Depas. Finally, he shines in a six-hour ride on the track at Charleroi. The liberation is total. Suddenly everything works, effortlessly. Flup jumps at lightning speed on the overnight train to Paris. The showy new industrial city of Turin sets up a world fair to rival neighbouring Milan. There will be a coura-geous plane race over ten stages from Paris over Rome to the Fiat grounds. Peugeot commissions a stage race for cyclists: the three-day Paris-Turin with stages across the Alps. The race formula is new and challenging; riders will start separately each morning, in reverse time order of the classification. The French Lion manufacturer is renting an impressive area of stand space at the industry fair. Peugeot then places a big order for champagne, has fine biscuits baked and invites important people. Marketing mix and VIP villages are of all times. Aviators for the plane race arrive on 15 July. En route, Rolland Garros (French aviation pioneer and war hero whose name will be posthumously linked to the Open French Tennis Championships in 1927) has crashed with engine trouble against Tuscany's reddish pulp earth.

A day before, the three-day Paris-Turin cycling race started in Paris. Stage one is 322 kilometres to Dijon. In a sprint apotheosis, Thys pulls ahead of Salmon. Philippe smashes his wheel faster than his seven-year older compatriot. The Walloon is hefty fondman and formidable climber, but fortunately not a sprint bomb. First chasers Figuet, Bertorelli and Garda trickle in ten minutes later.

The next stage takes the riders to Geneva. The innovative start system means that Thys and Salmon virtually leave together for a short ride of just 195 kilometres. Yet Philippe strong Félicien cannot keep up and has to allow two minutes. Most competitors leave much more time. For overall win it goes among Belgians. Thys knows he has until Turin to close a couple of minutes. That should work. It is a viable: catch up with Salmon as fast as possible and wait until the line to beat him once more in the sprint.

Everything goes according to plan. Salmon is a climber, but Thys apparently climbs even better. It is exactly seven o'clock Italian time when, at Corso di Francia, he fist-balls the stubborn Namurois back with great strides. Thys navigates between a mishmash of gelatis sniffers, gesticulating cops and balloon sellers, straight into the arms of Monsieur Robert Peugeot.

Two of the three rides are in. Flup proves how well he can master the pro distance: without weakening. At the inauguration in the new stadio, of the neighbouring Crosëtta district, a mega-heavy bottle of vermouth awaits. It's a trifle compared to the Alpine cols.The city dignitaries then fly the loaded and jaded trophy animal furiously around the neck afterwards. Didn't Nietzsche - in Thys' year of birth, no less - fly a beaten horse comfortably to the neck here, for a close embrace? A figment of Dostoevsky's novel Crime and Punishment.

Thys' win is woefully real. A short stay awaits. The Mole Antonelliana tower and the studios of the film industry - of which Turin is then the capital - invite. It is reminiscing and letting fresh memories sink in. The trip through the high mountains with its glacial silence have impressed. The pure air particles, which generate power and make pushing uphill for an eternity so magical, have been a discovery. Of the explosive coffee sweets: a kilo for home please, or make it two.

▲ Winner Philippe Thys on arrival of Paris-Turin for Indépendants, 1911.

1911

Impressionism

The spirit of discovery, in which young painters at the time sought out nature and plastered real colours and striped light, gets a sporty variant with the Circuit Peugeot-Wolber. In this Tour de France for the promising, hundreds of riders are let out like young cocks. Together they take refuge in an adventure story, undulating on their physical limits.

The first edition in 1910 proved to be a huge and enthusiastic hit and was more akin to an exploration of benevolent towns and bucolic scenes, than a cycling race. With as many as 526 riders registered, they visited 14 stage towns over 3,000 kilometres. 316 survived a month's tour of France. Guénot had turned out to be the best and had a great future ahead of him. Henri Pélissier, who would win the real Tour de France in 1923, was third. Regardless, the clean story should get an extension in August 1911. Over 16 stages this time and preferably with a little less and better people. The clockwork round of L'Auto is over. A sober grocer's son finally became overall winner thanks to a regular cadence, although all the attention went to the second. Paul Duboc was left poisoned on a haystack. Cyprien (Gustave) Garrigou, as overall winner, was beside the point. Good thing the Parisian from Pantin can now celebrate his moment de gloire. Soon he will bump into Monsieur Philippe. From then on, winning may not happen. Desgrange writes of Thys' first Tour victory that the Belgian showed extreme regularity, a quality only approached by Garrigou.

We are nowhere near that far. Thys closely followed the exploits of the major champions in July. On 4 August, it will be his turn. Confident and well in his skin, he is ready for the first decisive assignment of his racing career. The man from Brussels

◀ Philippe Thys upon arrival for the Circuit français Peugeot-Wolber.

wants to show that he is the distance runner of the future. The Circuit Français Peugeot causes a stir even before the drapeau de départ goes down. The French Cycling Federation decides not to homologate the race under any circumstances. The organisers admit riders who are serving sentences or have overdue fines to settle. It is no longer possible to spoil the fun of the young crowd.

Thys's angriest rival will be Gabriel Figuet, from Hauterives near Valence, today beyond the dreaded Lyon. Crowds are foreign to the Drôme department in those days. The region is a collection of humpy purple slopes with the occasional cricketing slow village and framed Vooralpen on the horizon. To prepare for and live in a big stage race, it is prime terrain. Figuet has already proved in Paris-Toulouse how strong he can be for the day. He is a bit of a strange flake. There are plenty of those in his hometown of barely a thousand souls. Postman Fernand Cheval is there at the same time laying the last stone of his unreal Palais Idéal: a massive accumulation of rocky material considered one of the most remarkable expressions of naive architecture. Half a lifetime earlier, fascination has struck, on picking up the first lump of rock. His palace will become a national monument.

On 2 August 1911, Thys has his bicycle laded at Avenue de la Grande Armée, while latecomers are inexorably sent home. They can participate again next year ... if they learn to be on time. The world is artificially Spartan in those days.

At 6 am, 320 participants are ready in Champigny. August 1911 is approximately one of the hottest months of the census. Between 4 and 20 August, the mercury peaks above 30 degrees for a fortnight. Up to 40 in the south and even 35 on the Atlantic coast, where ocean breezes, however, always enforce coolness well inland. The kick-off is for home rider Kippert. He gets to ride solo into Nancy in sultry lightning air. After the rest day - which follows each stage - they trek over the Ballon d'Alsace like the greats. Figuet gathers lead points.

At the Peugeot factories, on the road to Chalon, all 8,000 workers were given an hour off by Monsieur Robert and Monsieur Etienne. Over as much as three kilometres, an impressive hedge of spectators with banners forms: a goose-bump moment. On the Côte de Maiche, Thys is with them and makes a successful bid for Jura stage win. Chavière remains leader and Figuet is close behind. Heading towards hideously hot Clermont-Ferrand, there are kilos of nails on the road. Philippe miraculously escapes the sharp.

Meanwhile, people in Paris are dropping dead and charriots are sinking deep into sticky melting macadam. Bursting thermometers do not stop Castelain from mounting a huge raid with Tiberghien. The Belgian gets sunburnt, but the Nordist will persevere to the line. That's why Thys

▲ Supply in the Tour Peugeot-Wolber, 1911.

is only second. He does a fine job in the standings, though. The exhausted bodies cannot catch sleep. The mercury never drops below 25 degrees. This must herald the end of the world.

Immediately, that final verdict does not come. At four o'clock the rooster crows and a moment later the doors are banged. On to salty Bayonne, where a second bouquet is waiting for Kippert. Philippe is up to speed and takes back the four points he foolishly lost to Figuet in Perigieux. Chauvière is still well in the lead. Until he takes a shortcut in Cathar Land and has to pack his bags. Thys does not improve. He gets wheel breakage and will once again despair. A chat with Sicat brings back the moral. This pimply 15-year-old is still on the race, on a heavy bike with

ordinary tyres. He has to manage everything himself. The truly secluded, relying on the goodwill of the people for daily bread and bed, will have a tough time. Between Carcassonne and Nîmes, France presents its worst roads. Regional Falandy has to shake off white dust and push off rabid supporters at supplies in Béziers. They stuff his bag full of fruit and sweet. When they want to quickly bring another live pack, the tired good soul suffers a tantrum.

Vallotton - second overall a year before - comes to ride at the front. Flup knows Leon from the Paris Veloclub Levallois. Another Swiss resident of Paris stirs up: Egg rides strongly. But he remains harmless for the classification. It is the champion of punctures. The unlucky rider constantly sews inner tubes while sitting cross-legged, his bike stretched out on the road. Figuet is different. He has ridden the Circuit a year before, radiates power and runs an extra point ahead of Thys. It is even hotter along the sea than at the Centre. Although the flanks in the hinterland of the Azuren coast hurt considerably, five of them storm towards Nice.

Figuet is eager again: deviates from his line and pits Vallotton against the finish. He wins by ten centimetres on Thys, but after complaint, the stage winner is dropped to last place in the leading group. Philippe is the new leader. Leon is secretly thanked. With a glass of local génepi, the little brother of absinthe? Now the goodie may still be poured. The combination with lingering tropical air puts the riders KO.

In the distant city of lights, attendants at the Louvre accidentally discover that the Mona Lisa has disappeared. According to angry Figuet, Thys is the thief on duty. He wants to enforce his displeasure and drop out of the race. The threats make no impression and Gabriel has no choice but to pedal towards Valence with the 143 others. Everyone on the home front is expecting him, with or without leader's papers. Will the annoyed southerner set off fireworks along the way?

The 380 leaden kilometres up the legendary National 7 scare. Drawing times at checkpoints are extended and the slope of Grasse gratefully taken on foot. Under a sweating sky, Egg wins. The persistent wins. The men for the standings take a big day off. It drips. Slowly at first. Suddenly harder. And even harder. A downpour during the hefty apero at the Mairie's expense cools the sour bodies. A carefree fresh day's rest on the spot saves half the peloton from destruction.

There is no need to leave the morning after the rest day until eight o'clock for Clermont, city where the eight-shaped course passes through France twice. The pendulum concept gives a more complete Tour de France feel than Desgrange's grand Tour, which only searches the contours of the country. Unleashed Egg takes Rondeau on a long flight. Within sight of Boulevard Cergovia, the Helveet takes off alone. Thys suffers another puncture within sight of the finish. It costs him points. Figuet takes the lead again. After the pompous punsch d' honneur, greedy Egg falls ill. He will not start again. Vers Poitiers, the caravan darts through the Limousin and the Gironde, where the tasty cows Egg so after can sniff the vines. Thys wants to force the race and runs out to six minutes, but towards the end Engel joins, to beat the energetic Belgian in stade Poitvin. Figuet has buckling knees on the day and only comes in 11th. As a result, he suddenly faces a six-point gap.

As Georget wins Paris-Brest-Paris, the 119 remaining young hulks rush to cycling-friendly Nantes. Now it is Figuet's turn. Thys feels weak and soon loses touch. Aided by outsiders, the Frenchman pushes hard and wins the stage.

Philippe finishes on nine minutes and gives away points. The Provençal's deficit is three dashes. The tambours and clarons wake the peloton as early as four o'clock in the morning, as Brest is waiting far kilometres away. Engel, Huret and Goethals go on a day's ride. At Vannes, Thys is leaking, at Auray again. Figuet stays put: tired after yesterday's raid. Thys is still five minutes behind in Lorient. Will the race tilt after all?

Rain brings rescue. Figuet catches sight of a pastor's splash. He is trapped and care-fully slides along through slippery villages. Taking more risk is out of the question. The threat is over. Well and truly back on board the keur group, things go wrong again for Phlippe at Daoulas. But he is ironclad and calm and rejoins even before they cross the wide waters of L' Elorn.

In the group sprint for fourth place, Thys - intrinsically faster - still crawls over Figuet. Two hard-fought bonus points fall from the screeching sea air. The trip along the Laval bend has little to show for it. The heat is back. Goethals wins again and Thys, in third, again gets fewer points than his rival. Figuet is on autopilot, clinging on but running out of fist. The road to Paris and 6,000 Francs is open. One more early rise. It is already very hot that third of September. In a nervous starting hour, 35 kilometres are advanced. A leading group of 32 greys wriggles through as many as 10,000 spectators, completely clogging up the Alençon horse market.

At Dreux, Thys recovers a pneubarst: too fast and not properly. A second puncture follows. In furious pursuit, it goes wrong again: puncture three. The stock runs out. He has to go on the gente until the next town. Panic strikes again. While putting in new stock, he encounters Figuet, who is also recovering. Sun has no pity. Both think only of brotherly riding instead of fighting.

Enough is enough. Versailles, the côte de Picardie, Saint Cloud, the bridge of Puteaux. Valloton or Leuvener Lauwers? Either one is sure of winning the final stage. The Swiss is a bike length better and Thys arrives third at the Porte Maillot 15 minutes later. The western gate at the Bois de Boulogne, at the time the sacred terminus of all famous races. Just under 100 lucky people make it to Paris.

The overall winner gets to take the top podium with 75 points. Figuet, 14 points richer - but that was precisely not the intention - stands next to him. Valloton climbs the lowest step. After sunset, Alibert will charge red lantern Reboutier 2001 points. The musicians of L' Algérienne play the Belgian national anthem in front of an international stage. Thys could be a big one, though that is no certainty. Belayer Figuet will never break through, for lack of northern sagacity. The Swiss painter's son will never even become a professional cyclist.

The International Cycling Federation is suspending all riders who rode the Circuit Français Peugeot. Fortunately, it is doing so wisely.

In order not to put the UVF completely in the wind, they effectively pronounce penalties that start diplomatically in October and end on 2 November: between road and track programme. Very briefly, a rumour circulates that Thys will quickly pick up a pro licence to ride the Giro di Lombardia on 5 November. Those who know Flup know better. All in good time.

▲ Gabriel Figuet

▲ The Circuit Français Peugeot-Wolber could count on a lot of public interest.

▲ Philippe Thys after finishing the final stage of the Circuit français Peugeot-Wolber, 1911. He had just won the Tour de France for independents.

1911
Cautious chicken-eater

· ·

After a week of welcome rest in Paris, the winner of the Peugeot Round returns to Belgium. In Brussels, they will have to be patient. Thys first picks up starting money in the velodrome of Liege. On Monday evening he will arrive at the Gare du Nord, at Place Rogier. The railways are not helping. The train from Liege is delayed and the dignitaries waiting neatly at platform six see the champion enter on track two. The reception committee is duly confused and has to do stairs.

Shouldered by his supporters, Philippe stands face to face with hundreds of revellers, flashing photographers, dozens of flags and bengal fireworks. The two policemen on duty at the station exit call for assistance. The Anderlecht Attractions association has put together a celebration in seven hurries, some overlooked. The internal order department makes the best of it. With a large banded Hommage au vainqueur du Circuit Français at the head of the procession, it heads down the city boulevard towards the home congregation.

Flanked by mom and dad, Thys stands upright in a fuming car that narrowly makes it to Place Bara. In their wake, a trio of associations step up. These outdo each other in the size of the gerbes. Under lanterns, flags and garlands, the procession dances down rue de Fiennes to the showy town hall at Place du Conseil. Alderman Crick has to excuse and replace the ancient mayor. Mayeur Moreau, as a councillor, is already in the front row with him when the communal pride is inaugurated. He has been in command of the municipality for more than 30 years and has even been sitting around the regulars' table at Het Klein Eiland, former mayor Van Lint's pub, when the first plans for a new Flemish renaissance town hall are unfolded. Ma knows them piece by piece, the politicians past and present. Crick was born on "'t

Eiland" (the island). Van Lint's cradle was in "'t Klein Eiland" (the little island) on the Mierenweg. At the Paepsemmolen of moilder Rieke De Potter, there was another tavern with the witty name Het Eiland Sint Helena. An uncle by marriage was a grinder on the grain mill and his son Lomme became a beer brewer. Mother Thys wanders off in her thoughts. But when speakers Lemmens on behalf of the inaugural committee and Varlez on behalf of the sports press, thicken the eulogy to her son, she is once again on her feet. The wine of honour is poured and eagerly drunk. It is time. The zegestoet advances to rue Wayez, finally settling down in the Poly hall, recreated in an arc of colour and fragrance.

La Dernière Heure newspaper ends the following day with: la salle tout entière croule sous un tonnerre d' applaudissements. The exuberant supporters flush with beer from Le Cygne and the occasional music turns sharply ...En kende gei the daughter of Maree Planché in. And how does Thys feel about all that? He politely and engagingly thanks everyone and enjoys himself from afar. After a festive tour of Anderlecht's Joermet, Brussels Sportif put on another banquet at the end of September. Civet de Lièvre façon Thys, is printed with golden curls on the menu. Philippe stores calories and again consumes few words. Emotions are expertly channelled into determination. Champion behaviour all round. The robust fellow has discovered his thing. He is at his best over long distances and hardly gets worse as the rides progress. He can conserve energy, keep calm, sleep well and tolerate the heat. That scientific theories can be successfully applied, he actually already knows. That there is such an immense advantage to be gained when a race is long, he has just discovered.

The Thys family has been given a sporting body by mother nature and it is being passed on willingly. Little brother also gets on the racing bike. He will become a more than decent racer. Guillaume also possesses a great engine, but for some illustrious reason he does not make champion fuel. Brother's perfect blood circulation will then be passed on to daughter daughter Josée.

After WWII, as captain of the mythically unbeatable Atalante Bruxelles, she celebrated the championship title eight times. Joseé Thys was called up more than 100 times for the Belgian selection. She is indisputably the best basketball woman in the country until the arrival of Ann Wauters. In summer, Philippes niece is active as a javelin and discus thrower. That too yields several national titles, but women's sport is too local in those days to dream of an international career. Sports literature has also completely forgotten her.

In contemporary cycling books, people portray Thys as an eccentric. Getting some-one out of bed in the middle of the night and onto a bike sounds fantastic, morbid and marginal at the same time. Grafting customs from then and now onto each other may make for a fun eccentric factoid, but current readers will be taken by surprise. In the Thys years, getting up very early is no exception. In May, the sun comes ready to scatter as early as four in the morning and the electricity-less citi-zen pulls up from the moment nature lights up. The German occupying forces only introduced the new time - popularly known as summer time - during 1916. Actually, in occupied territory, they set the clock to Central European time, making the sun appear later. Unlike our neighbouring countries, so-called summer time is main-tained in Belgium until 1940. The oil crisis of the 1970s brings the clock artifice back into the news. What really explains the extremely early surge of activity at the beginning of the 20th century is the mechanism of time zones. From 1 May 1892, Belgium ran on Greenwich Mean Time, much to the chagrin of Brussels, which had gladly stayed 17 minutes and 29 seconds later. The young Thys and his competitors were certainly operating simultaneously, at the crack of dawn.

Until 1916, the sun rises two hours earlier in summer than it does later. Staying in bed is not done among the common people. Fancier races are ridden in the early hours of the early market and the big classical races are shot up at night. How else could they have finished over 300 kilometres of bare road? Inns fill up as early as nine o'clock in the morning on Sunday; with all the consequences. At that time, the pigeons have already fallen and the men have already harvested the vegetables, so the women can get to work.

Philippe may already be a morning person and benefit from it, but much more important is his interest in strange living and exercise attitudes. He immerses him-self in dietetics and does interval training. A cyclist remains an exceptional figure in those days. Depending on the origin, it is a je m'en fou-tistic dandy with caviar traits from mundane pioneer sport or a peasant bear out of category, who eats large struts (West Flemish for sandwiches) and sucks up to two dozen eggs before the start. Either way, what both types have in common is defying the human body. The flogging must be incisive and overall.

Thys does not have a trimmed moustache, supposedly to reduce drag. Actually, because to a racing driver it is a dirty carpet, getting in the way. He practices essen-tially out of competition, barely rides races, denies himself centimetre-thick pork lard on daily bread and is sparse on alcohol and sweet, excluding gingerbread.

An ascetic type, Philippe becomes a calibrated metronome after his dealings with members of the Veloclub Levallois. Once under the spell of Paris, Philippe is even more concerned with what to eat, how to rest and when to train. The millimetric daily schedule is rarely deviated from. From a little after four o'clock until around ten o'clock on a training trip. Reading and perusing letters, midday meal and siesta. Then taking a long walk on the outside, walking and sometimes jogging, via 't Eiland near the Zennebroeken and over the sas van "'t Rad" - where a new workmen's quarter is under construction - to Aa's farmyard, the Zuunbeek and 't Negemanneke. Occasionally the trip goes straight on at the lock, along the canal to Ruisbroek. Sometimes there is a ford into the undulating landscape around Beersel. Philippe clears his head, puts everything in order in the upper room and walks until dusk. After a second refreshing wash, he takes a light and limited supper around seven o'clock -which is quite late for that time- and goes to bed at 9 o'clock on the clock.

After his 1914 Tour victory, Thys explained in an interview to 'L' Auto' what his success was due to: *"In the cold spring one should train, but not do any executioner's work. That is bad for the body. The meticulous preparation for the big tour starts in May. Then it comes down to executing the planned training programme correctly. No race one participates in during the preparation should be an obsession or an agreed goal. From Paris to Tours, it was nice and warm and I stayed in the lead group to add to the kilometres. As it continued to run well, I pulled the sprint for Oscar Egg and finished third myself.*

In Bordeaux-Paris, I went along until the point when the body told me to be good but not ready. In Paris-Vienna, I attacked on a short slope outside Arras. It was a testing moment where I had to see how long I could push through an effort. I eased up after a while, but they didn't come back.

Then I just kept going for 110 kilometres. I didn't lose a lead and didn't have to go deep. In that case, you might as well win by yourself. Paris-Brussels was on my wish list, though. I can do it at the beginning of June, because it completely fits into the finale of my preparation. But everything has to work out. After the control in Reims it started to rain harder and harder. At the border crossing, ice water even fell. I called sports director Baugé and got into the car with warm clothes. Had I continued to follow Mottiat, I might not be standing here today. The Paris-Brussels winner is still ill. As for the course of the lap itself, it's survival every day. Staying lucid. Looking ahead and assessing risks, observing the ground to avoid sharply.

Looking up again in time to avoid bumping into chickens, dogs, goats and long-horns. The French just let anything that lives on legs run free.

The peasant people themselves, are also dangerous. They walk along the road or cross like they are from another world, not even understanding that something is going on. I've only had one puncture in this Tour at a bad time. In the fourth stage to La Rochelle: when Georget was ahead and Rossius wanted to take advantage of my tyre change to set up a breakaway.

I never pass an opponent without taking as much as a metre away. If they pass me, I automatically swerve to the side of the road. It is incredible how often they stupidly fall. Losing concentration costs you effort every time in a stage race. We were given a whistle for the first time to send warnings on descents. Many riders laugh that off. I don't. So much for arguing against improvisation."

Philippe may already be cunningly careful: but that does not alter the fact that he too has broken a collarbone four times and has often been sidelined with bad luck in his youth. Even as a climber, Thys plays it safe and journalists are always struck by how bizarrely he tackles climbs. Powerhouses or opponents who want to stay on the bike at all costs, in places where it is almost impossible to ride, are given free rein. Philippe climbs more regularly, sometimes stepping off unexpectedly to suddenly jump up again. Setting foot on the steepest pentes is common then, not even a shame at all. The French ingineurs have not yet come along, to make the mountainside smoother and digestible for winter sports enthusiasts. Connoisseurs find little system in Philippe's climbing tactics. Yet the Belgian knows perfectly well what he is doing. Controlling the pulse to minimise slipping is important. So Flup clings on, trying to stay close and recover from bad moments.

Many ride until they literally fall over. The Brusseler sours more slowly and usually comes to the front in the last half of the race, only to be the best of the dying. When slumps occur, Thys immediately lets go, moderates pace, eats, drinks or stops and relaxes for a while until strength returns. He doesn't do anything headlong.

After arrival, he will rarely be seen hanging around the finish line. Ride in, hand bike to attendant Charles Deruyter, assume peignoir from père Bartélemy and be away with him in a vehicle to the hotel room. Immediately. No cold drinks, no uncontrolled eating. In short, the then most feasible version of the Protour team bus with recovery drink and washing machine. Converted to perfection.

1912

West Flanders cycle-horses

I n 1912, Odiel Defraeye is the first Belgian to taste a Tour victory. Cycling is once again frenziedly popular. West Flemish people have kept the race alive, in part by organizing bicycle races in the village center, from one wine barrel to another and back. The infamous Karel Van Wijnendaele, more commentator and jorunalist, threw cycling back into the national spotlight. He assembled the strongest riders and once the revival began, he gave his team of "flandriens" new challenges across the border. The plan: beat the French on their home turf...in Roubaix, via the Côte d'Opale to buttery Normandy and Paris.

Cyclists Catteau, Van Hauwaert and his companion Messelis, were hefty riders of what were shortly before - in local parlance - called veloce-peerden. These gag figures were the first compatriots to earn a living as bread riders. They lured the big French cycling houses to Belgium, looking for more of these giants, to put their homegrown celebrities, often classy but fragile, out of the wind.

The Flandriens are more willing to perform and cheaper than the French pacesetters. But sooner than expected, they discover their real weight in resounding coin. Les salopards demand a raise and threaten to ride on their own account. The untouchable team managements realise they had better feed the hefty cattle. By turning them into

◀ Odiel Defraeye overjoyed as winner of the 1912 Tour de France.

opponents, they are not getting anywhere. Brand advertising is always good, even if foreigners provide it. French public opinion, however, does not like the Belgians. Nationalism is rampant in those days, even with us. The young Belgian state needs patriotism and exploits to hang that feeling on. Defraeye will help. At the very moment when cycling resumes, Philippe Thys makes his entrance into cycling. Barely four years later he is a pro.

In 1912, Thys is already alongside the greats in Milan, following all the way to Sanremo. A heartbreaking moment: they can follow all the way. At that point, the Poggio is a grassy road that only donkeys can endure. The riders ride straight through it at an arrow-like speed. Sophisticated lads who know the entry into the Primavera town hit a small gap after a right-angled turn. Enough to stay in front. Flup is long satisfied and - ahead of Van Hauwaert - gets to finish 23rd. Insistence after a regrettable puncture in Cervo is no longer necessary. He fell once, punctured twice and at no point got into trouble. Henri Pélissier wins in the sprint ahead of Gustave Garrigou, Jules Masselis, Ezio Corlaita and André Blaise.

All in the same time. A week later, in the early morning of 7 April, the affable Edmond Proniez Thys hands over a large linen number 8, fitted with copper-plated pins. There is roll call at a quarter past seven in Chatou and soon they are off for the Paris-Roubaix hell ride. 164 kilometres to the crucial Doullens slope and then a good 100 to the finish on the velodrome.

Flup turns square, a condemnation to quietly cling on. Favourite Garrigou falls over a dog, bravely comes back with two broken knees, but will know his master on the Barbieux piste in home rider Crupelandt. The picking wounds are irrelevant. Gustave is an iron at the finish. Defraeye and Messelis are the first Belgians, at mere seconds. Twenty minutes later, the peloton cues into the sports complex. At the back, Thys and comrade Figuet dangle.

Meanwhile, Titanic goes down in icy waters because something is wrong with the climate. A winter at up to 15 degrees, follows an exceptionally hot summer that makes the eternal ice brittle. The drama makes for hideous drawings in the Sunday newspapers. Among the 68 Paris-Vienna participants who take in Suresnes, the sunken ship is the topic of conversation. The Paris suburb is another village with vines that have escaped the phylloxera.

It is gradually becoming the favoured starting point for cycle, motorcycle and car races, even though the small centre is locked in the meandering Seine. Here, too, they know what water can do. Suresnes barely recovered from the crue centennale. In the first months of 1910, the river rose to shoulder height for almost a month. Then it took another month to leave the Paris basin agonisingly quiet. Meanwhile, factories, slaughterhouses and coal-fired power stations were at a standstill and public clocks and streetlights were not working.

Get out of here. Flup is immediately in the right beat and drifts north with the leading group. The six of them blast through the deserted beet fields. Only a weeding farmer, using his clack light to wipe his forehead with, sees dusty riders turn up in the distance by surprise. He knows nothing else about them and will remember the riders only because a moment's pause with his head bared in sturling spring wind gives him a nasty headfall. Races should advertise a prestigious starting place and delight a large home crowd on arrival; what lies in between is entirely incidental. Thus the race docks on, through desolate territory. Before entering the velodrome in Menin, Philippe lets the others run. The sprinting contenders double him. Messelis smoothly points back Vandaele and Petit-Breton. At Alcyon, they will be happy.

The now considerably overgrown Tour of Belgium could become an important showpiece for Thys. In 1912, the stage race took in seven stages from Brussels to Liège, Luxembourg, Namur, Erquelinnes, Menen and Antwerp back to the capital. With stages of up to 250 kilometres, the national round shows maturity. In the opening stage, the sky Alcyon jerseys of Pélissier and Christophe and the tricoloured pride of Defraeye, turn the fiery Liège light blue. Through the Ardennes to Luxembourg, Pélissier and Defraeye make it another Alcyon party. In Namur: ditto. Odiel for Henri. Peugeot can't stand it any longer and leaves the round. Thys has already dropped out on his return from the Grand Duchy at the border, with a festering rump. The Tour of Belgium 1912 is won by Odiel Defraeye, a nice prelude to what is to come.

Paris-Brussels is going better for Philippe. After an early puncture, he is soon able to join a sizeable leading group. Neither the Charleville climb nor the ascending Meuse valley are able to separate the group. A sizeable peloton continues to climb for a long time past Overijse and Joli-Bois, until Stokkel and Weule. At the Haachtse steenweg junction, Thys is still in front.

Is his later love already there somewhere along the roadside secretly admiring the riders: one in particular? It's pretty much out of the question that the winged match-maker is already stringing up his bow there. Philippe's future parents-in-law move from Diegem to Schaerbeek in 1906, where father has a better commute. Mother Marie is from Anderlecht. Cupid certainly gets a second chance. Does Thys later, in the hustle and bustle of the Wayezwinkel-and after picking up some powerful pigeons at Menoenkel's inn-cross his future mother-in-law with daughter? He peering cautiously from under the clip of a large cap, she strutting back, looking back? Exactly as a first test of love should be: totally awkward. At the entrance to the Karreveld velodrome, a stressed-out gendarme horse also makes a clumsy move. The crowd along the side rushes apart and Flup loses all chances to be with the first ones on the track. He and Spiessens spend minutes prying apart piled-up bikes. Regardless, the test over 300 kilometres was successful.

The Tour is coming and the young Peugeot promising rider gets to go to Paris. The brand landscape is a bit of a mess that year. Alcyon has barely been on the market for ten years. In that time span, the particularly shrewd factory boss Edmond Gentil has managed to erect a brand new company building and increase sales tenfold in no time. Between his seething start as company manager in 1903 and the first Tour success with Faber in 1909, Alcyon already has a production line for 40,000 bicycles operational. They marketed mopeds with Swiss built-in engines - winning the world title in 1905 - and developed light single-cylinder cars. His French wonderboys, meanwhile, beat the Tour twice more with Lapize in 1910 and Garrigou in 1911. Now Alcyon, with Van Hauwaert and up-and-coming talents Mottiat and Defraeye, conquered the Belgian bicycle market in a hurry. Aggressive commercialism is Gentil's signpost. He signs monstrous contracts with the best riders and promises bonuses that make everyone giddy.

The established bike factories - even if they too are relatively young companies - do not know what to do with it. The great Peugeot has already quit its pro team to escape the absurd bidding. With a Circuit for independents in 1910 and 1911, the family clan from the East takes aim and discovers new blood. Even to that success, Gentil has a nasty answer ready. He promptly set up the Huit jours Alcyon in 1911, also to scout young talent. The media success of the Circuit Peugeot-Wolber, is cunningly contested by Alcyon. Daily and weekly newspapers are bought out, with advertisements under contract and the counterclaim not to feature the Peugeot races too heavily editorially.

The dirty play has a history. Edmond was once the apple of Peugeot progenitor Eugène's eye and, even then, a bright and cheeky youngster with exceptional commercial and technical skills. One day the two get into a heated argument. Ambitious Edmond wants to become director of the by-brand Griffon in Courbevoie. When the Peugeots want to hold off that boat for a while longer, Gentil pulls the door shut. Before that powerful slam, he shouts loudly: ...they will hear from him in Valentigney! Eagle-eyed Gentil - his pointed nose and chin omni-present - builds his own brand and later buys up La Française and Thomann, among others. These outhouses are allowed to keep their pro teams, allowing clever Edmond - if need be - to manage an even larger part of the peloton. He is always and everywhere one step ahead of the ball. The kingfishers (Alcyon is a fabled bird from Greek mythology) literally peck everyone's plate empty in spring 1912.

Those who buy up the best riders sometimes already have a luxury problem. Desgrange has limited the team impact to factory teams with five riders. Alcyon faces a difficult choice. Defraeye will stay at home. Odiel is the figurehead of distributor Richard Bonte, who has spent thousands and thousands of francs to get the brand off the ground and profitable in Flanders. The Flanders lobby is threatening to terminate contracts for duzende and duzende velos and is getting even.

Paris cleverly deflects being bitten in the sand. Gentil never loses. Odiel can tag along, as first helper to outgoing winner Garrigou. There is always sports director Baugé: an inventive orator who reads the race like no other. He has a solution for everything and then an even better-sounding explanation. Yet another golden move is in the making.

▲ Above, Henri Desgrange as a cyclist (on tricycle!) and on the right as boss of the Tour de France.

1912

The Little Belgians

At the start of the tour of France, as many as 20 compatriots are lined up, eager to get in on the action. Belgium is ambitious in science, steel and architectur. The nation straightens itself, confident and complexless. Thys does not like that political fuss. He is mostly standing up for himself and coming to Paris to quickly learn the stile. The Tour celebrates its 10th anniversary on 30 June and starts at the Lunapark. His Peugeot-Wolber mates Salmon, Buyze and Deruyter look a bit stricken and wavering, like insecure cubs coming to stroke the warmth of popular leader Petit-Breton.

Tour boss Henri Desgrange has decided that 10 branded teams will be allowed to enter only five riders each, supplemented by 81 so-called isolates who will have to complete the tour without the support of a factory team. To highlight the ethics of individual sporting performance, Desgrange specifies some new rules. From now on, people will be allowed to help each other team-internally on a limited basis in case of bad luck. However, waiting for a teammate who has fallen behind or handing your bike over to an unfortunate mate is not allowed. The liberating articles of the Tour Regulations read like a sieve and are full of full sentences, which can be read from front to back and vice versa. The possibility of interpretation remains high. The use of a bike with pion libre (freewheel or bulge that allows the legs to remain still) is allowed for the first time. However, in some flat and windy stages,

◀ The peloton in pursuit of Christophe and Buyze in the ninth stage from Perpignan to Luchon.

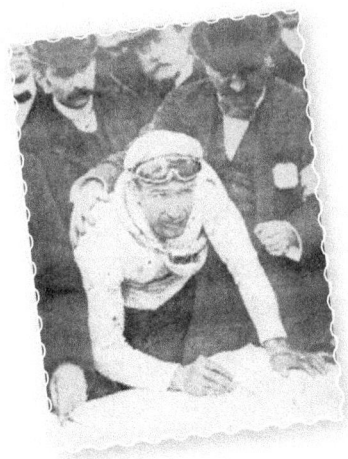

the free wheel remains prohibited because otherwise riders would forget to pedal too often...The classification will be recalculated anyway based on a points system. It will be the last time.

Crupelandt, after his home victory in Paris-Roubaix 1912, may also win the first northern stage of the Tour as a bonus. As in previous years, the roads of northern France are again littered with nails, much to the despair and annoyance of the riders. They cannot all be accidental lost nails. Wouldn't there be tactically strewn tyre punctures among them too ? Garrigou knows all about it and explains the technique: from a certain agreed point, the rival team scatters nails on one side of the road. Its own riders know they have to ride there on the other side and those who are not aware or attentive will puncture If all teams adopt this dubious practice you get general misery and flat tyres squared.

Favourites such as Faber, Duboc, Lapize, Georget and Garrigou fall hopelessly behind. Defraeye remains immune from bad luck and awaits Garrigou. Odiel has not been recruited to excel at this Tour. He just has to assist Garrigou as a super-manager and help him on his way to another Tour victory. Defraeye puts himself in the lead and the duo begin a kilometre-long chase. Team boss Baugé soon realises that Garrrigou can no longer get ahead and orders Defraeye to ride on alone. On points, it's simple: every place counts. He finishes 14th, far behind Crupelandt. Philippe Thys completely drowns in the hustle and bustle of the first stage and finishes 28th.

In the second stage from Dunkirk to Longwy, Odiel still has to wait for Garrigou again. The Frenchman still enjoys protected status. Fixed pay and bonuses are not insignificant, but it is gnawing at the superman. He is better than the black Gustave and finely flouts the Alcyon instructions. He drags Garrigou in his wake to the finish and sprints to victory. Garrigou beaten at the finish. Borgarello takes the lead in the classification. Philippe Thys finishes handsomely fourth 11 minutes later in a group with Christophe and Spiessens. Peugeot loses all its leader Petit-Breton in the Champagne region, having collided with a cow.

In the stage over the Ballon d'Alsace, Christophe is the better rider, but Defraeye becomes leader of the general classification. Thys is never very far. Flup makes

▲ Defraye wins the second stage in Longwy.

▲ The Italian Borgarello

▲ Defraye, Mottiat, Christophe and Alavoine
climb the muddy Aubisque on foot.

▲ Octave Lapize and Odiel Defraeye.

himself noticed for the first time, latching on to the front guard and even return-
ing smoothly after bad luck. He finishes 13 minutes from the winner, knocking off
another Félicien Salmon on the line. When the greats fezzle and send Faber out to
come and ask who you are, there is a future. Or did that story come rolling out of
the journalist pen that had to fill an extra column in extremis? The Luxembourger
is a good-humoured chap and certainly the sort of man who would compliment the
plucky Brussels man. But is it possible that a then top driver did not know the winner of the 1911 Circuit, a great promise for Peugeot's factory team?

From Belfort to Chamonix, Eugène Christophe does his thing again and snatches a point from Defraeye. They are now joined by Lapize on a handkerchief in the standings. Thys arrives in the company of an Albert Dupont, a fine guide with terrain knowledge. They lose half an hour, but Flup plays it safe.

Then come the tough jobs. To Grenoble, Aravis, Télégraph, Galibier and Lautaret await. Already on the descent of the first col, Defraeye encounters a quadruped and goes down heavily. With stabbing pain on the rotule (meniscus), he has to continue. Odiel is thinking of giving up. Pushing on one leg is lagging and there are still three cols to go. Fear of failure strikes. It's not running at all. Fellow countryman Firmin Lambot snorts past. He is in good form and reaches the top of the Lautaret swiftly. His thoughts already on a fresh pint, he carelessly begins the descent. After a while, it dawns on him that not a living soul is to be seen. The first passerby makes much clear to him: no, this is not the road to Grenoble, this is the other fork at the top of the Lautaret to Briançon. Firmin is dizzy, turns his bike around and climbs the Lautaret one more time. Finally at the top and finding the gap to the right descent, he meets dejected Odiel. Lambot takes pity on the young dying swan. As a routine rider, he knows that discouragement makes injuries worse than they are and that the Tournieuweling will regret for a lifetime that he did not persevere. The Walloon can cheer him up and keep him on the bike. Closer to civilisation, Thys also joins in. He is on a roll after his particularly good seventh place in the fourth stage to Chamonix. Christophe wins in Grenoble after 300 kilometres of rush hour riding. Lapize follows close behind. The two Belgians let Defraeye ride away at the end, fearing complaints. But Desgrange's gendarmes are everywhere and Thys gets three points penalty time. The Belgian damage was contained. Defraeye finishes ninth and even miraculously remains co-leader, along with Christophe. Lapize is still third on one point.

As a newcomer, Philippe does not feel the need to play cavalier seul. He joins to look around and make friends. In hindsight, he throws away four potential podium points in Grenoble. The home front makes its presence felt. Thys is well pleased. The little one managed to survive the series of a novice race in Sint-Gillis Brussels and finish eighth in the final run.

More or less recovered, Defraeye duels with Lapize in the next stage from Grenoble to Nice. It is a life-and-death stage race, to the point of amicability and exhaustion. Lapize wins and comes level in the standings. Now Christophe is behind. Defraeye's effort avenges itself just a day later, on the way from Nice to Marseille. Odiel swerves and tumbles into the ditch. It is there that Thys and Vandenberghe see him lying there. They think it's over and assume Lapize, like a bullfighter, will gracefully administer the death blow. But the Frenchman can do no better himself and narrowly follows the mob at the front. That Defraeye belongs to the Alcyon stable is no impediment. The bigger cycling can get in Belgium, the more honours and francs to be had. Fraeye is refreshed, helped straight and put back on the bike by the duo. Odiel comes out on top thanks to a generous helping of champagne. In Cassis, he gets the leaders back in sight, and in La Ciotat, they actually connect. Marseille is on fire. Army and grèvists play cat and mouse in the city centre streets. Sailors throw fish and when the baskets are empty with harder stuff, until the city stinks like a rubbish dump. Progressist and white Algerian Chanot, soon after, can become mayor again and clean up the mess. The Tour arrival is wisely shifted, outside the city. Lapize has lost north and snaps mentally, when the Belgian - without even realising it himself - wins the ride on the bargain. On an uphill road, where nobody knows exactly where it ends, mad Defraeye gathers all his remaining energy. Lapize dares not follow. He has wasted his chance to make a move. Now he has to finally take it himself and concede points again. That gives the final blow. Not yet on 14 juillet to Perpignan, but a stage later. Heading towards Luchon, in the scorching heat of the midi, motorised Octave gives up, exhausted and dehydrated. He sets off for a climb

▲ Faber and Buyze in the fourth stage Belfort-Chamonix.

and suddenly retraces his steps towards Saint Girons. There is no point in continuing if all Belgians ride for Defraeye and their French brand bosses stand idly by: reads the defence. That same evening, Lapizes' entire La Française team quit. The French sporting world is utterly shaken when more bad news rolls out of the telegraphs. World star and aviator Latham is killed during a buffalo hunt on America's great western prairie. Odiel's closest rival Christophe, has also lost out and is already trailing by 20 points.

On stage 10, from Luchon to Bayonne, neo-pro Mottiat works his way into the spotlight, beating Christophe and then falling off his bike from fatigue. You shouldn't expect anything like that from Thys. He is not on the podium in any stage. Yet the Peugeot debutant is always around and, after his bad day in the Alps, is climbing steadily in the standings. In the lee, half actor and half spectator, he only occasionally cautiously pokes his fierce nose at the window.

To La Rochelle, the ride history is disappointing. Sprint bomb Alavoine can beat a big group there that kept pedalling alone on the way because there was no other way. Thys places fifth. In Brest, Louis Heusghem cheers. On his second Tour entry, he wins his first stage solo. Defraeye has time and excess. He follows at more than half an hour. Thys has a dip and is almost two hours longer on the road. In 16th, he again loses places in the standings. Odiel is now 32 points off. Towards Cherbourg, Alavoine comes up with another sprint number. Vandenberghe, Defraeye and Thys, have to resign in order.

In the fourteenth stage to Le Havre, speedster Alavoine grabbed second place again in a bunch sprint after Borgarello. The brave Frenchman is creeping closer and closer to Buyze and Thys in the standings, in fourth and fifth place. In the point final in Paris, everyone is looking forward to the battle for the places of honour. Philippe - a bit à bout de souffle - lets himself be beaten by Alavoine, who takes his third stage win. A fourth place in the final stage is not enough for the Brussels rider for consolidation and Buysse also shivers over the finish line. With 147 points, he will hold off the pushy Frenchman by one mere point. Odiel and Alcyon decisively win the Tour: 49 against 108 for Christophe on bike Armor and 140 for teammate Garrigou. Of the 131 competitors, 41 reach the finish.

Defaeye's reception on the home front is never seen, the madness total. Bright Karel Steyaert - until then a contributor to the Izegem Sportvriend - sees the chance to make his dream come true. He will play a leading role in a new sports daily. The very first Sportwereld on yellow paper will be sold that autumn during Koolskamp Koerse as an advertising stunt. At the same time, Ernest Van Hammée, previously already director of the velodromes in the Bois de la Cambre and at 't Molenbeek Karreveld, announces that his sports palace on Brussels' Avenue Bertrand will be ready within a few months. A stability problem due to the swampy ground, is finally delaying the Schaarbeek opening by several months.

Mottiat is the greatest Walloon promise for years and with the publication of Velo-Sport (later Les Sports), Alban Collignon once again gives French-speaking Belgium a reliable sports magazine. Home-grown cycling buzzes and churns from Ostend to Arlon. The reception of the first Belgian tour winner is huge. Odiel travels all over the country and gives every compatriot a hand, a wave, a kiss, a look... On Wednesday 31 July it is Brussels' turn. Via the avenues of Tervuren, it is off to rue de la Loi and the Nord, with Van Hauwaert at the wheel of a long limousine. Whether Thys is also in the area is not known. Was he allowed or required to accompany him to the federal seat and the celebration at the Hotel Métropole? He is not a public man. Longer than strictly necessary, he will certainly not have stayed.

The 'ket' (nickname for a Brussels inhabitant), who has shown great things as an enthusiast and independent and has been taken in by the talent scouts of the French

▲ Eugène Christophe and Louis Mottiat, winner of the tough Luchon-Bayonne ride.

▲ Honoring Odiel Defraeye in open car through Brussels.

cycling houses, is happy to be on the fringes for now. 22-year-old Thys has his first Tour de France behind him. Nowhere did he make a spectacular appearance at the front, but in Paris, thanks to regularity, the somewhat mysterious boy from the suburbs did place six. Even closer would have been possible. As a first-year pro, he meekly carried out employer Peugeot's assignment. But through measuring and weighing, he has also received confirmation that he can dream of more. With a bit more daring and focus in the initial stages and a year's extra corpus, there would have been room on the podium. The eight points too many, came mainly due to lack of terrain experience and knowledge of one's own limits. Modesty is not the problem, let that be clear to all. Thys is made for lap work. Before and after, he weighs 68 kilograms. Defraeye loses six pounds, Buysse as much as 10 and Alavoine has even thickened.

Philippe does not fail to forge the iron, even if it is lukewarm. With Vandenberghe, he turns on the 24-hour race at the Karreveld track. One wants to try out a variant of the French Bol d'Or there. The 24-hour endurance race with pacesetters captured the imagination in those days. The race was created in 1894 by Frenchman Decam and paid for by later Tour sponsor Chocolate Meunier. The name refers to the gold-plated bronze winner's trophy.

Brussels showers cause frequent flagging off. On Monday, the rain stops and den Bol starts again. But not for long. A drizzle sets in once more. At the popular velodrome in Zurenborg, they expect a packed house on Antwerp Mother's Day, at half-time. In a meeting, Thys meets Tour hero Defraeye and very often has to hold back and play comedy to let the exhausted party animal do his thing.

The intoxication stops during September. Pà is not well. Hasn't been for a while. Things are moving in a bad direction. Leaving contracts on the table is not an option. At the reopening of the Sporting Palace in Ixelles, Philippe cannot be missed. Van Hauwaert lashes out heavily. Thys is not used to the poorly lit indoor stuff on bobbing wooden slats and takes a tumble in the early stages. He gets 12 revs against his ears. On the night of Friday to Saturday 5 October, Desiré Thys dies, at home, rue de l'Agrafe. Father succumbs to the effects of double pneumonia, barely 46 years old. With the offspring working and flying out and him and Ma having a carefree roof of their own over their heads, there might finally have been the prospect of peace. Everyone had still urged him to get that lingering cold treated. Always been so tough and athletic ... Flup immediately cancelled a meeting at the Arsenal in Gentbrugge.

▲ Philippe Thys after arriving at the 1912 Tour de France.

1913

Anti-favourite

L'Auto announces a revamped Tour for 1913. For Henri Desgrange, attention to his course is vital. L'Auto sold 14 million copies annually in 1903. That number tripled to 43 million by 1913. The popularity of the Tour is his life insurance policy. Credibility and excitement must be safeguarded at all costs. The abandonment of the full La Française team in 1912 lay heavy on the stomach. The zest and ambiance was gone after the passage of the Pyrenees. There were no more stories up for grabs to lure readers to the newsstands with. The points system clearly played havoc with the sporting event of the year. A ranking with time differences should provide more tension. The role of Desgrange, judge and party, also raises questions. Will little shrimps and driver-vedettes get equal treatment? Organisers will allow three independent race commissioners from the Union Vélocipédique Française and post official timekeepers at the finish. Prize money will once again go up sharply. That's enough, then. Now everyone must shut up again for a while.

For the first time, the Tour goes counterclockwise: from the city of lights towards the west and Pyrenees. Then the Alps and Vosges follow. The riders may use the pion libre more often: except for the ride along the Atlantic coast to La Rochelle. 5287 kilometres remains a tough assignment for the 140 participants (including 51 brand pros). With Louis Trousselier, Lucien Petit-Breton, François Faber, Octave Lapize, Gustave Garrigou and Odile Defraeye, there are six ex-tour winners at the start. Some teams number up to eight riders, while others are more limited in size. Armor starts only with Scieur and Heusghem. The contingent of foreigners is growing and becomes a potpourri of colourful exotics. The most attention is undoubtedly given to Neffati from Tunisia. At 18 years-and-a-half, Ali is the youngest ever participant in the Tour. He became happy owner of his own bike two days before the

Paris exit. Attacking and admirable during the day, the tanned boy is also a sight to see after the stage arrivals. His acrbobate tricks become daily newspaper fodder. In 1914, his precious bike will be smashed by an official on the way to Luchon and the North African will be allowed to climb the remaining cols as guest of honour on the cosy back seat of a car. That discovery caused him to opt more often for the flatter piste work from then on.

The Belgians are not left behind and, in turn, innovate cycling. Van den Haute and Van Wijnendaele design the first Tour of Flanders for their sports newspaper De Sportwereld and Brussels, like Paris, will hold meetings and six-day events in a permanent sports palace.

At that very moment, Philemon Vanden Stock cut his first blends into bottled Lambic, as Geuze was then often called at the gates of the Pajottenland. The young brewer sets an empire in motion with a few second-hand devices. On a second front, a club of Anderlecht boys in purple and - against the dirtiness of the short knee-breeches - black football gear, celebrate the stepping up to national football. They want the municipality to give them a respectable pitch on the local Meir. To that municipal park, Queen Astrid will soon lend her name.

That both fait divers as befits lambic liquid will be adulterated into a grandiose sporting distillate sounds utterly ridiculous in 1913. The genie is also completely out of the bottle on the bike front. Peugeot has gone on the attack. Trustee and

▲ Gustave Garrigou, winner of the 1911 Tour de France

manager Leopold Alibert, who was part of Valentigny's furniture, has left for Automoto. That's an uppercut. Alphonse Baugé - mastermind behind Alcyon's sporting success - is bought out and reunited with the reliable Luxembourger Faber. That one cheats, in retaliation, at Automoto. Garrigou and Christophe also don blue and yellow jerseys. For the distinguished Peugeot fraternity, they have had enough. Those who, for years, did not get involved in dirty dealings, on the contrary, worked with the youth circuit on a plan for a new generation, bite back. Alcyon in particular has gone over the top from the start.

Others decided to follow this course of action. Now Peugeot is reacting forcefully. Transfer fees, riders' wages and prize money are important and sensitive matters, but perish into thin air when the horse Prince Palatine changes hands. A South African mining magnate quacks the record sum of 45,000 pounds sterling on the table, enough to buy up the Tour spectacle several times over.

Poulain Philippe may quietly prepare for the round. His season gets off to a fine start. On the Côte de Pecq, just after the start of Paris-Roubaix, Thys puts everything and everyone on the line. Still on the front row in Amiens, Flup dropped out of the race in Arras when thunderstorms threatened. He just had to open the debates. Peugeot wins with Faber, in the best time ever measured over the course. Lightning bolts and roars punctuated the quick win.

There is no Thys in Tours, Menin or at the end of Bordeaux-Paris. He will not take part in the first Tour of Flanders on 25 May. Flup has travelled south, to explore the cols with Peugeot mates. A reassuring postcard arrives in Anderlecht. Literally on the sidelines, brother Guillaume receives encouragement for Brussels-Liège. The youngest does well in the indé classic. He finishes handsomely seventh. Is there more Thys on the way?

For the classic of the two capitals (Paris-Brussels), Peugeot drums up all its Belgians. They are sent into the black hole a little past midnight in Villiers. Back to where they came from. Thys starts quietly, crosses the border in the leading group at Heer-Agimont and, from the graceful and fashionable Wépion, is suddenly no longer competing for the marbles. Lambot, Duboc, Godivier and Scieur are also off. Stopped for early strawberries? La Française-Diamant packs all the clean prizes. Winner Lapize is already munching on his second Merchtem chicken, when Thys comes in 17th and last - an hour and forty minutes from the winner - on his way to the airport of Sint-Agatha-Berchem at leisure. Is that where the interest in rigs with wings is growing? Soon the Tour will start: is it from not being able to do better or is Flup throwing sand in the eyes?

From the Circuit Dinantais, no one will be the wiser. There are barely 23 starters. It is a Peugeot affair in which Salmon is allowed to pull away for half a minute and quiet Thys then beats Van Ingelghem for place two.

The Belgian championship from Charleroi to Philippeville - a week before the Tour - is quite uphill. Now there are valid opponents in post. The name of the arrival place will trigger something in Thys, write bland journalists without inspiration.

Flup does what needs to be done and casually rolls across the finish line as the last of 12 leaders. 8:34:22 course may suffice as final practice run. Joseph Vandaele stands shining in black-and-yellow-red. Philippe does not care much. The focus is elsewhere. The same day - over the same route - the youngest clocks 13th among the independents. In Anderlecht, they are moderately satisfied. But is it enough to compete in the Tour?

At Peugeot's boring pre-meeting on the eve of the Tour start in Paris, the riders are allowed to express their expectations at the end of the meeting. Garrigou, Buyze, Christophe and Faber are all formal: they want to win. No one flinches. Baugé suddenly looks Thys in the eye. And you, what are you thinking about, because you never say much: asks the cunning team leader. Thys would never have applied it himself. Now that they ask about it, he is momentarily confused. When no one is expecting a reply, the confession follows: I also think I can win the round. A silence falls. Then irritated legs shuffle off uncomfortable chairs. Finally, murmurs follow. Marcel Buyze - a powerhouse who always and everywhere, wants to challenge everyone, including himself - sits down right in front of Thys and speaks: if thou even now thinks thou can win ...schen Brusselere ... then I have nothing to fear.
Mutual curiosity is piqued. Thys and Buyze will regularly share the room during the Tour and often hang out together. They are each other's opposites: the restless rake versus the calm expert-comptable. It is this perfect interaction that keeps both mentally fit during the rest days. Pastimes and post-race relaxation have nothing to do with the race itself. On the bike, there are no gifts.

The 1913 round has a difficult start. Flagman Abran is ill, has to cancel and does not want to pass on his pennant. Of course, the false note doesn't really compromise the retreat under the lanterns of the Champs-Elysées.

The first stage goes classic to Le Havre and ends equally classic in the sprint. Italian Micheletto trumps a bunch of Belgians. Jules Messelis takes revenge in the next stage. Petit-Breton and Defraeye drop off cursing. Brest also prepares for a sprint duel. Fraeye has to let a jumping Pélissier get ahead. The topic of the day is Lapize's stylish abandonment. Octave was the man in form in June. French championship and peerless in Paris-Brussels. He was up-and-coming for the round, but steps into a bistro and sits with his back to the window. As the riders pass, he gobbles down a copious meal. I am always on my own within La Française and have to earn bonuses only to share them with lazy teammates. Then I'd rather ride on the track on my own account: shares the national hope sec. A despondent Desgrange sees Lapize's angry teammates disappear from his course after the tricolour jersey. Georget, Crupelandt, Brocco and Duboc no longer start, after barely 40 hours of Tour fun. They are all crowd favourites, selling papers in their region. Defraeye is in the lead again, but what on earth can L'Auto do with that. A new great player, Marcel Buyze, ranked barely four seconds lower, is blowing hot breath down Odiel's neck. And Thys? He didn't get off to the best start and has already had quite a bit of tyre trouble. Picking up 22 minutes is not nothing.

▲ Riders at the start of the 1913 Tour de France.

▲ Flemish Tour pioneer Cyrille van Hauwaert in the company of sports director Baugé and in the background the starting flagman Abran.

▲ Jules Messelis

Buyze continues to spew energy like a dragon until he snatches a victory. He succeeds in La Rochelle, under the watchful eye of Defraeye, Mottiat and Thys. These are happy that the pounding can stop for now. Marcel gets ten minutes of penalty time for unnecessary wheel change. His fury is not over. With day's win for Vanlerberghe, the Belgian arsenal of powerhouses seems inexhaustible. His victory as an islolé makes all sports archives around the world go tilt. Ritten starts 15 minutes later than the grouped branded teams that day, but can ride to the head of the race with Everaerts without anyone noticing. In Bayonne, they only have to sprint among themselves for stage wins. After all, by regulation, they are 15 minutes in front.

Buyze, who once again wins the sprint from the leading group, is angry and initially doesn't understand a thing. Then - in Johan Boskamp style - he well-nigh squeezes the deserved winner with a good laugh.

Thys is still 22 minutes behind Defraeye at the foot of the mountains, slightly behind Christophe and Buyze. He has done no foolish things and feels excellent. Over Aubisque, Tourmalet, Aspin and Peyresourde, he does not let go of the strongmen of the first week. During the closing lanes of the Tourmalet, Thys is in the lead, with Christophe in his immediate vicinity and Buyze a few corners down. Before the summit, the Frenchman struggles and loses footing. In the descent, he will smash into a car exhausted and break his bike fork.

▲ Ritten Van Lerberghe   ▲ The retreat of Odiel Defraeye.

Eugène is cuit. The slump has everything to do with the way he and Buyze, for two climbs, have been riding leapfrog constantly. They have worn each other out and wrung each other out. The Frenchman has to look for a recovery site on foot. Le Gaulois happens to be a metallurgist by profession. That immediately casts a fainter light on the exploit to come, which will subsequently become the most staged story in all Tour history.

Eugène is a handy Harry and single-handedly manages to get his bike roadworthy again, under the supervision of troublesome commissioners-controllers. Christophe est un homme aimable: always helpful, good-humoured and positive. This makes him the exception within the world of elite athletes. But l' homme noble has already lost the Tour the moment he is on foot and has to walk up to the blacksmith. The tour de force performed by the French favourite rider at the bellows in Campan will be magnified so fiercely that everyone will attach de facto merit to Tour wins.

That Thys quickly lost a difficult opponent on the desolate Tourmalet, no one can deny. In the list of windfalls, Defraeye's abandonment is also fantastic news. The outgoing winner is suffering from a hip injury, but he needs to start the Tour and show himself. This works out extremely well at first, but the mountains are too much. In Luchon, where Thys eventually arrives with an 18-minute lead, Odiel is nowhere to be seen. Soon after, Ludovic decides that his Alcyon team will drop out of the race. With the departure of that coterie of rapaces voraces (greedy birds

▲ Eugène Christophe   ▲ Mardel Buyze

of prey), Desgrange has fewer problems. They have occupied his lap long enough. On the road to Perpignan, Buyze is clearly the better of Thys and arrogantly claims the lead. In the pouring rain, on the col de Port, Marcel solves with everyone. Thys arrives at 12 minutes, third, behind Paul Deman.

Buyze - obliged to go through life as Buysse due to a clerical error by the

town clerk - goes on a rampage. Against the strong bonk there is little to do at that moment. Philippe must secretly hope that his companion falls off the road somewhere. The giant mocks everyone and everything and drives for all premiums. He always needs pennies. Marcel spends what he earns, faster even and it may already be a bit more. Tomorrow he will push hard again, to pay today's debts. Baugé, psychologist and new team manager at Peugeot, has already had to talk in on many cocos. On Buyze, he cannot get a grip.

Marcel is all-powerful and god in the depths of his mind. Until the evening after stage 8 it is announced - it had been hanging in the air for days - that he has to accept an hour of penalty time. Buyze does everything that is not allowed, constantly colours outside the lines and constantly gets licked, but is still ahead. He runs into time penalties and fines every day, but appeals and then asks for staff reduction as a last resort. Marcel knows the rules all too well. Rather than comply, he also plays cat and mouse with the management. The commissioners get caught up in their accounting. They set Buyze's counter to zero and recalculate all the staff reductions and extenuating requests to finally arrive at a weighted verdict.

Thus, attentive Thys sneaks up to within two minutes in the standings. Only on the way to Nice does Buyze's cable really kink. As the reckless Flemish rooter continues to challenge luck so much, a stone of obstruction lies ready at the bottom of the fast sink of the Esterel. The nugget comes from Cheval's stone temple near Valence. Figuet single-handedly rolled it out to sea to jeer Thys within sight of Nice. There, for the southerner at the time, prospects of fame were lost for good. But the plan fails, as Marcel is already back in front and in his invincible mind the rock will give way in 't past. Buyze's promising career ends there. Had it not happened with that deliberately misplaced rock, another one might have been waiting for him soon.

Steering failure is brutal bad luck, but his reaction is especially telling. Buyze sits in the side moaning and taking no action. Brave Christophe takes him in tow, after long insistence and palaver. They saunter as far as Mandelieu - today the quartier du gulf of Cannes - hoping to find a recovery spot there. But Marcel is no slouch at fixing bikes. Christophe assists him. With advice, with deed may not. Alavoine and Hostein keep waiting. Both lack courage, patience and insight for two hours. His obliging teammates have their hands full to then keep him going on the coast road. Alas. The sporting momentum is wasted.

Firmin Lambot wins the stage, ahead of Van Daele and Thys. Whiner Grooten Buyze makes it to Boulevard Risso nearly three and a half hours from the stage winner, disheartened, and wants to go home.

On the rest day, Desgrange has other concerns. The fiercely depleted field still has 33 riders, including 17 individuals who see their chance to ask for an increase in the daily rate. The tour boss folds. Anything is better than having to ride through Paris with an invisible mini-ploton. He wants to spare the Tour that embarrassment. The Mediterranean also has pleasant events in store. Petit-Breton sees his mother again for the first time, having made the crossing from Argentina.

1913

The diabolic land of the North / 1

Buyze is being pampered and talked down to by senior Peugeot envoys. He will start again in the Nice to Grenoble stage. Well and truly out of the city, despair in his fickle head causes another big time loss. Faber precedes Thys that day. Philippe is 54 minutes ahead of Garrigou and more than an hour ahead of Petit-Breton. Buyze will banish the devils from his mind over the next few days, pick up the thread and pace everyone again. On the stage from Grenoble to Geneva, the fire-breathing dragon is back. Thys lets him ride off and rage for mere minutes. Out of ultimate precaution? Buyze humped all day on the offensive: from the Lautaret over the Galibier and Aravis to le Lac, arriving there barely three minutes ahead of Thys and Petit-Breton. Even the precise Helvets thought it was merely laconic cronyism. To Belfort, over the Ballon d'Alsace, Buyze shouts and rants like a drug addict. He shouts aside anyone cycling near him and storms up the mountain. The Boss is shocked when Marcel even crosses his car. Through rain and fog, to Longwy, Marcel does another great job. Two falls and a bent manivelle are the predictable result. Buyze again makes it to the finish line first. It gains a mere minute. Thys, who finishes fourth, still has an hour of comfort on Garrigou and Petit-Breton.

That he should no longer fear De Grooten will get further confirmation in the evening. The show-off is ruled out for allegedly deliberately driving in Faber's way. The hazy regulations plead à décharge, but everyone has evidently had it with the rascal.

◀ Marcel Buyze

Every day there is something going on with him. Buyze's punishment will later be overturned by the Union Vélocipédique Française.

On stage 13 from Belfort to Longwy, Petit-Breton tries to get away from the peloton. He still dreams of a third tour victory, to end his career in beauty. An hour behind Thys is a lot, but you never know ... break can happen to anyone and with this bad weather... Petit-Breton gets it right: Thys sprains his wrists in the descent of the Grosse Pierre. The wooden fence of a vegetable field full of rutabaga stunts his fall. Fierce gusts of rain break his solitary pursuit spirit. Flup gets a 15-minute loss smeared on his torn trousers. Petit-Breton loses narrowly to Faber in the sprint.

In the penultimate stage, to Dunkirk, Petit-Breton put everyone under pressure early on the day. Thirteen riders separate. Just before the faubourgs of Valenciennes, his Sturmey-Archer gearbox is acting weird. The chain twists into a knot at high speed and the cam wheel should lock. His Automoto creaks. The verhicel literally sticks to the upside of a cross chute and becomes catapult for whoever is on it. Petit-Breton cannot do anything against the basic formula of physics and goes over head. His bike literally lies across the road in three pieces. Lucien is still in one piece, but is carried with a fixated kneecap to the front door of a tiny workman's house. There they carefully hoist him into the best chair in the house. He will not get up again that day. From there the danger to Thys can no longer come. Philippe sees the Frenchman fall, but has no idea of the seriousness of the event. He decides that here is his chance to decide the classification once and for all. Even with an hour's lead, it is better to anticipate, for bad luck to come. Marcel Buyze begins one of his reckless operations over the cursed stones and Thys follows.

The region around Lille is an interconnected mishmash of workshops, ribbon villages, alleys and ill-judged street corners. Yet they race through the chaotic puzzle like madmen. Thys realises it is flawed, but gets carried away anyway. The people stand in the middle of the lane. This is where accidents still happen: ça passe ou ça casse. The gut feeling is right. Things are going wrong. Flup goes down in the tumult and becomes unconscious. A vicious splash of water brings him back to order. Merde de merde ... see that twisted bike ... He immediately realises that repairing folded steel cannot be done without suitable material. It is a secure job that takes time and must be done with care. If the bike tube breaks, there is even more wasted time. Helpful Christophe already drives to the control and has a professional called up. He briefly takes over Thys' computer and, with the vague approval of the orphaned Belgian,

▲ Philippe Thys during the ascent of the Galibier.

▲ Philippe Thys falls in the descent of the Grosse Pierre, and scrambles back up.

calculates a time penalty. When a velomaker points out the consequences to Flup, the latter is once again clear-headed: with your help I'll give myself another chance, otherwise it's over. What an immense difference from the Flandrien, who sat sadly in the roadside of the Esterel for a long time like a small child.

While the tenors lick or mend wounds, Marcel takes teammate Garrigou in tow. Does he want Thys to lose the round? To Dunkirk, it becomes clear that things between wild man Buyze and cipher Thys are no longer working out. That was different at the start of the Tour. Van Wijnendaele describes finding a pair of endearingly playful puppies in the room. Gentilhomme de nature Garrigou, suddenly does not say no to an unexpected second final victory. Unable to develop a pace himself, he hangs behind Buyze for hours flapping his arse like a dried-up tapeworm. Will or should Marcel take him to the finish? Has an agonising dullard risen in him once more? Is a whispering voice coming to tell him that he and no one else is the strongest and consequently gets to decide who will win the Tour? Or is Baugé comme précaution- in the dark about the consequences of the Lille rampage- already giving orders to save what can be saved? Surely Buyze can hardly return and leave Garrigou, at that point the best-placed Peugeot rider, to his fate. Meanwhile, Thys is sidelined for an hour and six minutes to fix the defect. He is finally able to start again.

▲ The passage of the Tour de France brings spectators everywhere.

Marcel may have ridden to the sea like mad, but once recovered, Thys takes 12 minutes less from Lille. The Brussels rider bites into his front wheel, unloads his good assistant Chistophe with a heartfelt sorry and, with the courage of despair, cleaves French Flanders in two. In Bergues, overlooking the port city, the Ch'timi, shouting that pti's leading position has been saved. Thys arrives in Dunkirk in 11th place, less than an hour from winner Buyze. After a late tyre break from Garrigou, the latter finally called salut and board to the

Peugeot support car. The commissioners meet long and late and do not show themselves. The comunniqué comes out alone: Thys receives a 10-minute penalty for third-party assistance. Garrigou approaches to eight minutes.

The minimum penalty has always remained a mystery. Desgrange could easily have imposed a double or triple time penalty. Did Peugeot get to decide for itself? The victory was for that camp anyway. Suppose they had given Philippe an extra ten minutes' penalty, he would have lost the Tour on the eve of the final stage. With paltry two minutes, decided by table-top judges as yet. Even Frenchmen among themselves thought that didn't sound right.

Jan Cornand, in his 1958 booklet Figures from the Tour, writes that the Brussels man had to weld his fork and went to work with Christophe in a forge. In that interview, did Philippe conveniently base his story on that of the oddball unlucky guy? Or has the author, after the contents of a bottle of peasant boys, mixed up juicy stories? A few paragraphs on, Thys says he was given an hour of punishment time for that, while that fine (it was only 30 minutes) falls on his head a year later. The interview is full of anecdotes, which, while rarely made up, are released time and again in a flawed Tour year. Is Philippe's memory a careless scrapbook? That cannot be ruled out, as his racing past is the least of his worries later on. Thys rarely looks far back. Van Wijnendaele let Flup have his say a few years earlier in People and Things. In it, the bad luck of Lille is linked to a pursuit of Pélissier. Again, faulty casting. Thys is always affable and acceuillant when someone comes to quiz him about his lap time. Refusing is not in his nature, but really making time for it and doing deep mental digging he does not. Ne kie zwanze and ne straffe stuut vertelle, that's what the press usually has to do. Then the diligent commerce man already has another appointment. In those days, things are not very strict. Stories have to contain lots and lots of drama. To question veracity, one relies on musty newspaper collections from hermetic libraries. Today a Youtube excerpt, via facebook would go straight to twitter and triumphantly punish the error. For suspens anno 1913, it makes no difference.

In the final stage from Dunkirk to the Parc des Princes in Paris, Buyze wants to show once more who is the strongest male and wins by a head start. En route to the city of lights, Thys keeps an eye on Garrigou's rear tube all day and regularly watches his. Nothing more needs to be done. Thys wins the Tour de France. Triumph!

Karel Van Wijnendaele has ventilated Buyze's bad luck on the Esterel for life as the reason for his loss. He does not take the inhabitants of Brussels, and by extension anyone not living west of the Scheldt, at face value. By deduction, only beyond the pernicious Ghent are true warriors born. Thys's compass has been towards France and the Ardennes throughout his career. The negation of Flemish cycling country could not be greater. He resolutely laughs off the magnified human flesh-eating spectacle. The editor-in-chief caste lord wants to write only about tormented races.

There must always be glittering raids through fearful mountains or over hideous rocks, to near death. When it is not hailing ice balls and lightning, he sets up a sprinkler of his own for the film set if necessary. These are elements the Brussels native rarely, if ever, uses to make his move. In his old age, Thys declares that the rules of cycling are simple: whoever arrives first without false strokes wins. What press or decorators ask and see along the way does not matter. Spectacle is not necessary. It doesn't buy you enough... and underpaid circus performers are pathetic people nobody cares about anymore.

Philippe is numerically addicted, saving up strength everywhere and getting carried away. That go-along system, means he rarely chalks up. Pedalling he only does when it delivers and he has the certainty that others are souring like pumpernickel. Signs of weakening in a big round are very often the result of unnecessary effort, delivered in the wrong places. Many lack reason and wit to use energy sparingly. The temptation is always great to go in on the feeling of good legs, cheering crowds along the road or the pat on the back from the Tour boss, who just wants to sell an exciting gazette.

▲ Faber, Garrigou and Thys arrive at the vélodrome during the final of the 1913 Tour de France.

Getting rich was in a rider's reach before WWI, but it was not in his genes. In excusal, it must be admitted that calculated efficiency and foresight were not taught back then. They are un-Christian themes, easily misunderstood as concrete steps towards laziness or emasculation. In a scarcity economy, one has to pick and eat the casual fruits of the day. Buyze, to cite a good example, again he, wins the final ride to Paris, only to go on the boom for three days unbridled. Purely hypothetically, only one person would have been able to understand and offer help to godlike Frank Vandenbroucke: Marcel Buyze to years of wit come...

▲ Arrival of the final stage of the 1913 Tour de France.

▲ Thys wins the 1913 Tour de France. Triumph!

1913

Anderlecht champion!

After all he is told and read, Philippe does not want a national welcome. With the witticism: did I actually ride, because I don't remember it very well, he smugly sends a message into the world. How outrageously biased most newspapers have been. Pulling Buyze forward like this and sweeping Thys' efforts between the folds on a daily basis.

In Belgium, Marcel remains the great hero and - like Defraeye a year earlier - is driven around everywhere. A few days later, when as many as a thousand high-class rulers gather in Brussels' Magdalena Hall for a grand banquet in honour of the Tour heroes, one has to come to secretly inform King Albert's envoy that chief party pig Thys will remain absent. Allegedly held back abroad, on business. Other sources put Thys in the pleasant plush of the Déjazet, theatre hall where a Brussels pièce-montée runs. Le mariage de Mademoiselle Beulemans does not make Flup any more agreeable afterwards. He is angry. That the Flemish gazettes are headlining even causes community squabbling. The national association of sports journalists, recently established with much fanfare, is not doing too good a job.

On 4 August, the Tour winner will return to Anderlecht, rather than to Belgium: by the side door of the small South Station. Once again, Flup has gone for a stage race in Liège first. Anderlecht is not letting it get to its heart. A market singer has been selling The Song of Thys for days beforehand. Cocardes and photos in three sizes

◀ Philippe Thys with the victory column at the arrival of the 1913 Tour de France.

are available at the station. These also hang in front of many windows and there are horse-drawn carriages ready for the Tour winner and his family.

On Limnander Street, thousands of people and as many as 50 local association boards wait. To Bara, a truck hands out candles and wick sticks. State guards on horseback open the procession. Five brass bands step out, including the Biestebroek society, of which Flup has been a member for years. Drama societies portray the past round.

The procession can leave. Mother and grandmother, brothers and sisters take seats in the carriages. Next to the winner sits Eugène Christophe, brought from Paris. In Belgium, the Frenchman immediately redeemed his status as the unluckiest of all those born before the accident. Aldermen Crick and Lemmens and Varlez again address the guests.

A new Anderlechtois wins a stage in the Tour of Belgium for independents that afternoon. He still speaks unintelligible Zelzaat. René Vermandel will become the second cycling hub and run a popular sports pub there, where weekly races leave for distant Flanders and deep Wallonia. Starting in Brussels will give the municipal race true classic status for the narrow-minded home front.

Across the canal, the party continues for Thys. After a stop at the Chapeau Blanc, it's uphill to Scheut, where an inn hall has been rented out. The flowers are down to the street. Getting to the spot, there is barely room for people. It is all pretty and engaging, but ideally Philippe would have liked to see someone standing in the doorway. Perhaps too weak to witness the whole victory parade, but here waiting to take his son in his arms.

Father sadly did not get to see his son win the Tour. That chief jay would have liked to cherish Desiré together with his champion and die afterwards if need be. The family must move on, with the blessing from above. They must get better together and be proud of what so much has been saved, practised and sweated for. After the sporting, let the riders talk about money-making often enough.

Olympic non-committal is by no means the attitude of the rider from the late pioneering years. The media put the riders' earnings into wonderful equations with much accounting abandon. The prestigious and expensive sports magazine La Vie au Grand Air, calculates what they earned at the 1913 Tour. Philippe is a tough businessman and knowledgeable cipher, but does he know that in the past Tour it took 80 riders to earn a franc?

With his supposed 25,000 francs in income, he can buy 50,000 loaves of bread for the family. A married couple in the factory, cannot earn that amount in their entire lives. Thys remains loyal to employer Peugeot, but soon wants to force better conditions. In the unreal bidding between the brand teams, golden deals fall through. Ask, you get. The bike manufacturers have the wind in their sails. Everyone tired of walking is looking forward to a bicycle. There are tens of millions more to go. Alcyon, Griffon, Peugeot, ... are the Apple's, Nokia's and Microsofts of their time. Thys may still have to try to make the most of it, given the madhouse full of cycling barons. Defraeye brings the solution. Called to Paris after a weaker season, he must do Gentil a favour. The latter doesn't speak the language, barely knows Flemish customs and doesn't want to walk full screen as the gravedigger of competitors.

Anyway, that is what brave Odiel is told when he is given the task of soaking Thys and Buyze. They can make the switch for a few extra pennies. That Buyze would be quick to take the money should come as no surprise. The Brussels man is a different matter: he thinks years ahead and knows damn well that he has to keep winning in order to receive enough bank notes even in the long run. Flup wants to talk, but he needs reassurance that he can go his own way at the Tour. Gentil - mad with glory - agrees. Thys will have to pay 20,000 francs to Peugeot as a ransom. Alcyon is willing to cough up that amount, subject to the counter-signing of a letter imposing double the fine, should he still dare to switch sides again. These practices are commonplace. Everyone knows that nobody can be trusted and that a seemingly unsurpassable bid can be followed by a much more punishing counter-offer. A bike had to be sold like a can of dog food today. Purely on sentiment. Consequently, there are several francs of publicity in the cost price. Consumer preference can only be achieved by giving the product a lot of added value. Champions in high esteem can do that best. There is no point in promoting superior metal or better wheels, because the buyer is anything but techie. That market mechanism, Gentil and Alcyon have grasped much faster than the somewhat stiff and mercantile-sounding producers of the first hour. They have since experienced that not participating is no longer an option.

Valentigney does what nobody thought possible yet: it buys Thys free again. Pure bidding. The big game growls and blows and makes itself even bigger to deter and impress. Who is playing poker the hardest? Thys himself. He won't let himself be ransomed again without a deal and without getting another piece of the better of it. Later Philippe explained: that he was very confident about the outcome, because a secretary and also big fan - read in love up to her ears - had to type out all the confidential correspondence and could also do fantastic eavesdropping.

Flup could thus gauge exactly how things stood and would never defect. He did business as he cycled: via one targeted robbery of the Peugeot family's wallet. Thys may be quick to tutor the Peugeots, look inside their lives, even stay at their châteaux on occasion and taste slow-boiled ortolan from their cleanest china, but he will always keep his distance. They remained his bosses, they did not become friends. They proved this several times later, by being unreasonable and invoking the slightest economic dent to take away everyone's agreed money. Flup rarely errs from camp. The Peugeots look like ordinary people, but they do live in a world that is not theirs. Together they have clean goals: always getting better and trying to dominate. Philippe may give way to contentment once in a while. Never for long, but still for a while. The Peugeots' drive never stops. They are always driving, to keep winning, but there is never a finish line. In normal social conditions, without insane war and austerity, Thys would surely have been safe for years.

At the hands of the 1914 winter contract, he was guaranteed to start as Tourkopman. Each new win would force him to take precautions and buy a bigger fire box. In life, trees were going to grow to the sky for Thys, rice pudding and golden spoons service compris.

That he didn't have to worry so much about his greed is proven by the Peugeot brothers themselves, after paying the ransom. With Alcyon now hanging in the ropes, the moment suprême arrived to hijack banknote-wielding Pélissier as well. So there was indeed enough for everyone, for Brussels as well as Paris.

CYCLES PH. THYS
TYPE
TOUR DE FRANCE
PARFAITS
SUR
PNEUS DUNLOP

1914

I raise a glass to myself

▲ Gavrillo Princip is net aangehouden.

Gavrilo Princip did not steal his name. He, and no one else, gives the starting shot of the 1914 Tour. The Bosnian Serb pops off the heir to the throne of the Danube monarchy in crab basket Sarajevo. The news does not immediately cause immense upheaval. Those silly Balkan tragedies: twelve in a dozen. 147 riders are on their way from Paris to Le Havre by then. Desgrange changes little to his recipe. The introduction of frame numbers on the bikes are just about the most important innovation. And whistles. Riders can use them on the descents of the cols, to warn spectators and other road users. For the first time, Australians are making a trip around the world to ride the Tour. Don Kirkham and Ivan Munro are doing so with verve and will finish 17th and 20th. This is in contrast to one Georges Goffin, illustrious man from Liège, who takes part under the pseudonym Nemo. Three times in a row he is first at the start in full livery and will each time abandon in the first stage.

Within sight of the sea, after thirteen hours of rotation, Thys sniffed the iodine deep into his nostrils and won the sprint from Rossius and a sizeable leading group in the streets of Le Havre.

◀ Philippe Thys before the start of the 1914 Tour de France.

– 105 –

In the stage from Le Havre to Cherbourg, the result is the other way round: Jean finishes ahead of Philippe. They ride away in the finale between the two of them and share the lead for now. Meanwhile, Europe is coming to the realisation that the political dominoes may be a bit too close together after all.

In the port city, Peugeot is staying in the same hotel as Jean Jaures, the great French opposition leader of the left. The politician is there to protect the common people from belligerent agitators. The riders have a chat with the stern figure while hopping down the corridor in adam's costume. Jaures, slightly indignant at first, then laughs his head off and zigzags down the stairs laughing: ces sacrés coureurs rigolos, des brutes sans gène.

It has been scorching hot for several days: riders, politicians and diplomats alike are suffering. On the way from Cherbourg to Brest, Georget and Thys tumble over each other on a descent. Immediately, the harnesses are back on and Peugeot orders some teammates to wait. There is nervousness and grumbling: fast, fast. There is no man overboard:.yonder they ride. Alcyon and La Française smell opportunities and turn up the throttle. Philippe has to get carried away by Baugé behind the backs of his mates. The head of the race gets out of sight. After an hour of chasing, not a metre has been made up. Thys gets on his hips. The Lion brand always wants to operate homogeneously and exude graceful cohesion, lubricating the we-feeling.

Valentigney has vision, unlike other teams, who bring in mercenaries every year and skim the interesting bargains like vultures. The lion has been drawn so many times backhandedly brutal by the tail that in 1914 it decides to bite off: clawing deep into the flesh unexpectedly. The model team is on the rise, but one has bought up more would-be winners and champions than is assimilable.

Actually, at Peugeot they are making the same mistake as enemy Gentile shortly before. Everyone now opposes the blue-yellows: they have become targets. Thys is nervous. Clean theories have to fall by the wayside for a while. He knows all too well that top cycling is only team sport at a moment's notice: when interests spur or extra money is on the table. Sports directors often pretend. They tear back and forth in robust follow cars to sprinkle directives around, but the riders then implement them within their own logic. Sports directors are above all a fine psychological as-set. Alongside and in the race, turning a heel on the opposition succeeds quite nicely. Understanding characters and playing or restraining each one to size is a plus. They

▲ Riders at the start of the first stage of the 1914 Tour de France.

even manage to get rivals who live under the same roof to cooperate for good or ill. That is where the sports directors' interest ends. Strategists in pre-war racing never become them. Thys knows only too well that while his teammates will ride on towards Brest, they are far from all sacrificing themselves. Nobody just puts all his energy on the reseau Peugeot, including Flup himself.

Too many cocks remain in the run in all teams. The envy is high. Their own stage win or a good classification opens so many doors, that they would be foolish not to keep thinking a little about themselves all the time. They sometimes ride like fools in those days, but they very rarely make foolish efforts for others. So catching up is not always a matter of ability, but also of will. For those who do not come to talk and serve butter to the fish, they do not ride full. So-called teammates, often bring top riders to bridgeable distance and then come to negotiate. The teams themselves, only throw out gold coins at the end of a stage race, to play it safe. In the early stages, they gamble along, as they usually have several horses in their stable. PMU horses admittedly, who often run ahead and do not line up. The peloton is a market square on wheels snaking through the landscape.

Thys ignored Baugé, joined the lead and closed the last gap himself. In that last effort, hostile followers come to sample him once more and blow clouds of dust into his dogged face.

Buyze does not leave it at that and runs away again that day. Still Thys is not safe. Philippe returns and Marcel grins: are you looking to win the round again Flup? The stage ends with a group sprint anyway. Emile Engel beats Buyze and Mottiat.

After Brest, the momentum wanes. In La Rochelle, Oscar Egg wins and Rossius-Thys remain ex-equo leader.

The riders walk through the French tropics. Along the coast to Bayonne, the Landes bring languor. Ham in sight and Egg could win a second stage in a row. Still, it will be some time before they reach tasty Bayonne. On the way south, the speed drops below ten per hour. Shaving, stealing drinks and taunting the peasants is a full day's work.

That the prologue of the 1914 round would flush so smoothly was an unexpected windfall for Peugeot. At the start in Paris, when director of sport and promotion Lemoine calls his bedraggled troops together to convey some community spirit, things do not look good. The man is searching for the right words that evening. It does not sit well. Everyone thinks Alcyon - with Defraeye and Buyze - is going to chew up the Tour and leave only scraps. Thys senses that the mood must be restored and suddenly raises his glass: to Peugeot. Many years later, Phillipe frankly admits that he was mainly thinking about his own second final victory and could use some help. By speaking so emphatically and boosting sizes, he commanded leadership advantage. Philippe is general of the troop. In the southwestern tip of the map, the tactics produced clear results. Defraeye and Buyze have already received several penalties and are trailing by an hour. They did appeal, but the mountains never lie.

On the rest day, Thys, homme pointilleux, explores part of the important mountain ride. He sets out early by car to explore all the mountain passes and decides to have the classic 4m60 and 20 fitted. The powerhouses pedal a metre more.

Pélissier and again Egg set out on the attack early on stage six from Bayonne to Luchon, with the four classic cols on the menu. At the top of the Aubisque, Thys passes nine minutes behind Pélissier and Egg. The duo take up to just under 15 minutes' lead. Then the Swiss rider unloads at the front. Girardengo, who has to play Italian white rabbit for Automoto, gives up. He has fallen numerous times in recent days and has just collided with a cart.

▲ Oscar Egg on the attack, on the climb of the Aubisque.

Lambot climbs the Tourmalet easiest , he joins Thys, accelerates and then goes to tap the Frenchman on the shoulder. On the Aspin, the Walloon is alone. Thys does not get the gap closed, but does cycle past all other competitors: eventually even at half an hour. Among the French, Pélissier licks wounds and Alavoine may still hope. Both are still in the front. The Alcyons are unrecognisable uphill. The Buyze brothers - Marcel has taken his younger brother Lucien under his wing - hook up at the first bend of the Aubisque. Lucien will make the route from Bayonne to Luchon his own, 12 years later he will win the Tour in this stage. On the flat, Marcel gives it his all before fiercely weakening again in the mountains. In the descent his daily spectacular tumble follows, costing time and money. Odiel Defraeye wanders sickly and listless along the flanks. The strength in his cycling legs is forever draining away. Thys is firmly in the lead. Pélissier follows at half an hour, Alavoine is another 15 minutes slower. Rossius has fallen through the ice, losing more than an hour. He can cross his podium ambitions.

Flup checks. No one dares to challenge him. These are dangerous words. Thys goes hard against the gravel on the next ride from Luchon to Perpignan, near Aix. Face considerably hit, he reconnects with grimacing difficulty. After a hefty gulp of Vin Koto made from Peruvian coca leaves, everything is back on edge. Some competitors swear by Vin Tonique Mariani, with the same basic recipe. Alavoine wins the stage in the sprint of Buyze, Thys, Pélissier and Rossius.

On arrival from Perpignan-Marseille, 24 riders are stopped at the Prado velodrome. The track is too small. A drop-off in series will decide stage wins. After a 370-kilometre ride, a small piste meeting could be off after all: or have the Tour riders become sissies? Philippe is already happy to make it to the finish and gets himself looked after. While finalist Lapize turns a blind eye to the finicky boozer Brocco. Joy and sorrow lie in a small place. The stage winner will leave the round. A macabre telegram brings the death of his mother to the Azure Coast.

Pélissier and Alavoine cannot wait to test the battered Belgian leader in the stage to Nice. This is a daring operation, as Thys is always in his element there. On the Turbie, everything still seems under control, but then Phillippe suddenly has to set foot. He bends over. Stomach problems. The opposition is also no longer giving a fresh impression. Defraeye has ulcers. Mottiat gives up. Buyze has to pick up time in the descent and crashes full on a motorcyclist coming up the hill. Bystanders fear the worst. It stays with broken fingers and a concussion. Marcel can no longer hold a guidon and has to leave the Tour. Jean Rossius provides Alcyon with a small success in Nice and still fights his way back to place three in the standings. Gentil carelessly tips the telegram into his dustbin: the news falls far short of expectations. Pélissier arrives with Thys and is promptly told that ten minutes of penalty time await. Such a decision is always good for the course.

The colourable rider takes revenge on Desgrange in the 10th stage to Grenoble. Thys initially slides along, but soon goes head-to-head. Overcoming the faintness and remaining calm as always, the Brussels rider rejoins on willpower. He sees stars but continues to cling on until the sweet Rhone valley beckons. In the sprint, Pélissier is faster than Alavoine. Lambot and Thys no longer sprint along. Moreover, Pélissier's penalty is waived.

Attention. Henri is on a roll. Thys is not yet rid of him. A straw man goes after Flup and offers a bundle of francs to let Pélissier win the round. With no response, the Frenchman again pushes hard in the high Alpine cols towards Geneva.Thys grabs his wheel with great difficulty. Pelisier is remarkably friendly and passes his drink can several times, but then the penny drops. And danceuse he taps Thys on the arm and asks quietly: isn't there some proposal you should know by now? Think again ... Henri doesn't even get a polite look and suddenly forgets to kick. If he doesn't get his way he gets mad. Mind you,I stand by: thought Thys was still quick to provoke, but he swallowed his words. Garrigou had nothing to do with it. He did not delay and won in Switzerland, ahead of Pélissier and Thys.

About the attempted bribery, Philippe kept his lips sealed and said he never knew who was operating behind the scenes. But that he kept a closer eye on his equipment and sampled all the follow cars that came near him as never before, he took for granted. Because Desgrange did not care about my story and the French had not won for so long: Thys did sometimes become a bit loose. Finally, he always closed the case with the telling: s' il n'ya pas de preuve, il n'y a pas d' histoire. With his statement about the lack of French victory, Philippe was clearly already mixing up time periods. In 1914, Belgian supremacy may already have been a nuisance for the French, but not yet a stigma. It is quite possible that Thys, in his evocative comments, was just riding some wave on the classical aversion to French arrangers. Even with the Tour boss, Thys occasionally peeled a furtive egg with the Tour, if he was given the right forehand to do so. Desgrages always portrayed himself as punctilious sports referee, but when it suited him, he could suddenly become the nonchalant champion of the French battle: the basset once let slip.

On the bike, the sinewy Frenchman Pélissier got better by the day anyway. On stage 12 towards Belfort, he put another map on the table. Philippe fits on the Ballon d'Alsace. His whole body aches. At the finish it is not too bad: sixth and two minutes lost. Special thanks to Rossius and Lambot, who catch him and sneak him into the wheels.

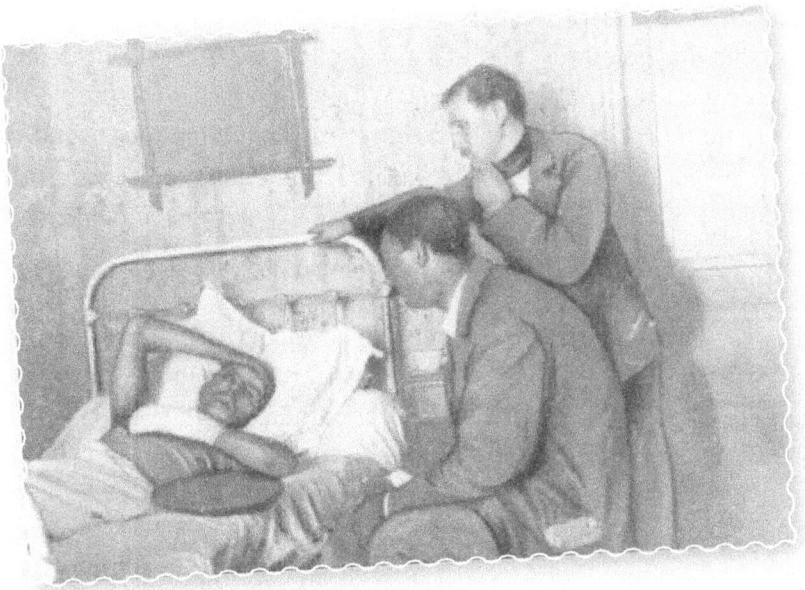

▲ Marcel Buyze is recovering from his bad fall,
but will have to leave the Tour.

▲ Faber, Garrigou en Thys op de Col d'Allos.

Philippe is getting through the difficult days. He is still more than half an hour ahead in the standings. In Longwy, teammate Faber always wants to win. The peloton meets the cavalry on stage 13 and they don't shy away. Coomans, Scieur - though in Thomann's cone orange outfit - and Rossius are the casualties. The soldiers do not even stop when the Tour insukes the verge. Within sight of the blast furnaces, Faber still meets the stern of a galloping horse-drawn carriage. Pure fatigue. He does not relinquish the seven-minute lead on Thys and co. that remains. The Luxembourgers cross the border via Differdange and Esch and rejoice with local picon au vinaigre blanc in hand.

Recalling 1913, Thys did not sleep soundly. The route of the 14th stage, from the three-country point near Longwy to Dunkirk, still runs along the cobbled lanes of the northern industrial area. The roads there are littered with potholes, bad repairs and train tracks near factories and asten. Bad luck lurks behind every bend and thousands of careless people jump around, starting the holiday many hours early with anything that can disinfect the throat against the killing poussière de charbon. It's looking out. With two rides to go, he has 31 minutes and 50 seconds ahead of Pélissier. At the slightest hitch, collected France will conjure something out of the tricolour hat. If Henri has something stuck in his head, he will surely go over the top to prove his point. That Pélissier and Desgrange don't give each other air to breathe is deception. If they see an opportunity somewhere, they will do anything to lower the Belgian flag and raise theirs. Thys is not religious and certainly not gullible.

1914

The diabolic land
of the North / 2

W hy the round absolutely still has to go to Dunkirk in the finale is a mystery. Lille could also have been done. Desgrange didn't think so. When Trousselier - the man Thys first called the basset hound - takes the lead, the whole peloton is in a huff. His trousers are worn through at the back from friction. He has to cycle home in his bare bottom. In Maubeuge, all the favourites are still together and Trou gets new clothes. Lille is approaching. Paying attention now. Thys starts riding a few metres behind the leading group. One now enters roads where riders often swerve for potholes and hook into each other. And then, in densely populated areas, there are always unstable hordes of cyclists who want to follow the riders for as long as possible. Letting themselves swerve a bit is a sensible move, but not a conclusive policy. In the vulgar crossroads village of Wez-Marcquet, another helping of bad luck awaits.

A vieillard saunters across the road between rows of spectators, as only a stubborn and potty-mouthed elder succeeds in doing. They shout him aside: de côté pepé, les coureurs arrivent. The leading group slides through in one piece. Then the old greybeard suddenly swerves anyway, on a bend. Thys, coming up behind, has only the brush as an escape route and goes down. Jumper torn, wheel broken. Non de djuu, soulârd, shouts Flup, selling the fool an unpleasant poke in the ribcage out of sheer frustration. The misery repeats itself. Heusghem gives his wheel and Faber drops out.

◀ Philippe Thys after finishing the final stage of the 1914 Tour de France.

In the turmoil, Flup forgets to take out the moyeu of the broken wheel - which has a control lead hanging from it. A race commissioner beckons for him to continue. The irreparable part is noted. In Hazebrouck, all is forgotten and they close in. That Thys would have bought a wheel in a shop, as is sometimes told, is fiction. In the hairpins of Casselberg, four stout climbers ride away. Philippe confidently takes the lead. His three companions puncture.

Pélissier closes in again. Faber is happily on hand and stays in support. The luxury rider from Luxembourg gets the win. At the finish, the friendly judge has lost his notebook and memory. The poor wretch has to yield to the tour boss, who whistles back at him.

Desgrange is formal: Thys subit une penalité de 30 minutes. The Belgian bursts with anger and defends with: Rossius made the same mistake a day earlier and was not fined. There are underhanded manoeuvres involved. The course management's reply flatly reverses the argument. Rossius' mistake was overlooked. De Waal still gets 30 minutes of penalty time. The bar is the same for everyone.

Thys's lead over Pélissier is still barely 1 minute 49 seconds. L'Auto can get ready to print a monster print run entitled: The Tour decided on the final stage to Paris. The wind is too strong against to put the announcement into practice. The two protagonists have little appetite for the promised duel. In the final stage from Dunkirk to Paris, the riders need two hours to cover the first 42 kilometres to Calais. At the control at the Café de la Plage in Boulogne, it is raining bladders.An impressive group of shelter riders arrive. The otherwise fought-over crayon aniline passes rhythmically civilised from hand to hand. Bauvais: an hour and a half behind schedule. Thys is lucky. It is windy and raining harder and harder. Escape is impossible. Pélissier is obliged to ride with his big maw - ahead of the leader - into the breeze and the drops. To ask for help, even at this hopeless moment, he is too haughty. Besides, who would want to help him? In Poissy, there are still 15 of them, and then Pélissier starts anyway.

He has to do something. Four riders pick themselves off: Thys on Henri's wheel and then Rossius and Brocco. That Pélissier makes another valiant attempt to shake off Thys in the hills around Paris, but dense crowds of spectators block the way, is a fable that did very well in French sports literature for a long time.

It is a desperate story. Le Coeur Volent is a short walled slope in Louveciennes near Versailles. At the time a narrow prickly diversions off the N186, a good three hundred metres of climbing. Thys wants to be careful there, leaving room to parry unforeseen bousculades. For more than a few lengths, Henri is never  ahead. Entering the Paris conurbation, there are already nine of them. Faber at the command.

Behind, as many as 500 fervent cyclists join in. When they storm onto the bridge in Saint-Cloud, the whole bunch hooks up. Everyone straightens up. Nobody gets hurt? No damage to the bikes? Thys' heart beats in his throat. Two kilometres to go. Finally. The contours of the Parc des Princes are becoming visible. They are going to sprint. Pélissier gets the final stage as a gift. The overall winner sits neatly in his wake, behind the shocking torsos of Wirtz and Rossius. That is Flup all over: no risk, no triumphalism and no need to upset French public opinion. But just remaining the best and making that gladly and painfully clear.

Thys rushes to make a statement. What happened yesterday was an attempt to mentally destabilise me, but it didn't work: clarifies the primus in one breath. The round ends on July 26. Peugeot has four riders in the top five (Thys, Pélissier, Alavoine and Garrigou). Alcyon-Soly has one rider left in the race: the fantastic Rossius from Liège who is quietly wriggling between the Lions.

About the finale, which went spicy as sambal and propelled the villagers into the streets, the winner many years later likes to say that after arriving, he stuck his nose right up against Pélissier's spiky beard. Even if you had ridden with me to and through the real hell, I would have kept following you. You didn't stand a chance, even with the support of the whole of France. Until next year Henri: sounded the bitter final words.

With his caractère de grand seigneur, Pélissier apparently still barked back: on points I am the best, with 37 against 46. Thys turned his back on that cheap subterfuge in a throwaway gesture with: then you should have won two years ago, now time counts.

Now, his win had not been so obvious. Philippe had cleverly solved the orchestrated vicious time penalty with special thanks to the stormy weather, but hard nuts were cracked in the Alps. Pélissier was clearly the better rider there. The racing bike of the as-yet deserved winner, was on display for days at the Maison Peugeot on Grande Arméelaan. Thousands stuck like flies against the display case to see the magical machine with the broken wheel up close.

In the République du Croissant- nickname for the Parisian neighbourhood where all the newspaper editors live- a fanatic attacks Jaures on 31 July. The opposition leader succumbs on the spot. A convinced pacifist, he had come to Brussels the day before to argue against the impending war. Jaures did not want to know that the very people who had no right to decide and no voice would shoot at each other. The culprit was arrested but later acquitted because he was doing a great service to the nation. How blind and cynical can a country at war be? The same day, France and Belgium declare general mobilisation.

On the morning of 2 August, Thys is picked up at North Station at 11 o'clock in a minor way. Pélissier has travelled with him, in view of some piste contracts. After a brief reception, the party is offered lunch at the Karreveld velodrome, where a first meeting was normally scheduled. So the hostility between winner and attacker is not that great. Gore pranks, such as bribery and coalition, are part of the game. Once arrived, the game is played. Everything may not have been erased and forgotten, at least temporarily put away.

An hour after the arrival of the final stage in Paris, Pélissier had to give an inter-view to Radio France. Thys - who, as the winner, got the scoop straight away - has just left the broadcasting room. Asked if he saw the Belgian on his way out, Pélissier gives the funny answer: non, car je présume qu 'il a toujours 1 minute et 49 secondes d'avance sur moi. There are many good reasons to put away the sporting feud. The overall winner asks his closest opponent to come home with him, to improve together. Extra people always show up for such duels and each puts a nice commission in his pocket. The grab-the-poon show does not go ahead, as the Germans enter Luxembourg unannounced the very next day and buy up all the remaining anime tickets. Belgium is in an uproar: den Doitch is suddenly eerily close. Belgians Forward d'hour has been called to go venge us: it sounds in the flagged streets of Brussels. The verbal aptitude contrasts sharply with the effective preparedness. There is not even a rifle for every soldier, not even a weatherproof uniform. No one has received basic training and the artillery can barely make 300 light cannons roar. Therefore, scouting Ulans cross the Belgian border without any fear. Meanwhile, 40,000 recruits refuse to enlist. The Belgian army is a collection of lead soldiers. Pélissier thinks his way and rushes back to Paris on the earliest train in seven hurries.

Il « Giro di Francia » 1914

1914
Pilot grounded

1 t the end of August, German troops seized Brussels without a fight. Columns pass through the Anderlecht main road for days. In all possible squares, the Germans set up field kitchens. They eat anywhere, anytime. The counters and cold stores of butchers are requisitioned. The butchers think it is a shame that all those beautiful steaks and rôtis are sauteed in a mixture of fat broth. Clean red meat one fries goo g'assaisoneit, anyway in a substantially buttered pan!

The Prussian foot soldiers have no manners. They challenge the population and take possession of everything. Soon they will lock up mayor Adolphe Max. Towards France, there are still stretches of no-man's land that can be easily crossed. The front is not stable and Paris perfectly accessible for those who know their way around and get informed. A few days before, Philippe says goodbye at home to all those he loves.

The army command tipped off during the homage at Karre Field. As a car owner, Thys had better volunteer. He may accompany members of the army staff in Belgium for as long as possible, driving them to the coastline as the enemy advances and piloting them towards England. That foreknowledge brings man and horse silently across the sea, while other notables are ordered to surrender their vehicles to the Belgian authorities mere days later. It is not long before Philippe is in Folkstone sweeping the consulate premises clean.

◄ Philippe in uniform.

His eldest sister has also fled in extremis and will find shelter chez cousine in Paris for the time being. The other Thys children remain at home. They are minors and French customs officials are being difficult about that. Survival will succeed; with American canned goods, bran bread of 't comity and meagre field fruits for which the fields of 't Potaadegat and the Vogelzang will be combed. Flup has left spare money to go into the black market with if need be.

On the home front, terrible rumours immediately spread: Thys was killed on the flight to England, Defraeye's body was found on the Rupel in a tranchée... One week later, half the platoon turns out to have died. There is nothing about it. France is stronger than Belgium and will hold off les boches. Paris will not let them take it away. It is safe there and the war will not last long. That's what everyone says. Thys is already making the crossing to the city of lights. But things will turn out differently. With his niece -une dame avec presence et de conviction who left oppressive Brussels for a Parisian varieté existence - he is soon locked in a golden cage. The war is not going away and cycling is at a standstill. A young powerful man cannot keep walking laps in the park. Friends-riders of Levallois are all heading to the front. The atmosphere becomes grim, even in the fashionable metropolis. What is a burly force in clean costume still loafing here? Why isn't this one going to defend the country? Thys reads it on more and more faces.

When the Belgian Air Force opens a training school at Etampes - an hour below Paris - in May 1915, he goes to have a look. Signing up as a volunteer has to be done through the recruitment centre and Belgian military headquarters in Calais. In October, Flup is called for a training session. After that, he can work as a mechanic at the air base. Tour winners don't like to wait. On 19 October, Thys walks into the meagre sleeping pavilion: much to the surprise of his future roommates.

He can repair a bicycle and knows the basic techniques of tubes and wheels. That is all it should be. An aircraft of that era is actually a bicycle with wings and an engine in front. The training school is a wartime enclave. The aviation men do not tolerate prying eyes. Nobody can give them orders, because at that time nobody knows anything about pilots and pilots. Flight instructions without a proper script degenerate into slapstick, in which rare and precious rigs already collide on the grass, tip over on their sides or later fall out of the sky. The French from the famous Farman school down the road, laugh their heads off. Flup is doing a nine-to-five job. The food is good and there is time to train. That too is allowed, as a great cyclist in the barracks is like a mascot. Camp supervisor and former cyclist Charles Van Den Born gives permission. But it serves to nothing. The world storm is still expanding. The Italians switch sides: it will make little difference. Commonwealth armies take beatings on the third front in Turkey and at home, more and more resistance members are executed at 'den Tir', a prison at the former shooting range near today's Belgian national broadcasting building.

In the summer of 1916, the war is locked, but professional cycling resumes with fortnightly meetings at the Parc des Princes. Behind tandems, Philippe wins by half a wheel from Ali Neffati in September. The Velodrôme d'Hiver knots up again with a grand overture on 5 November. Meurger - abandoned by Thys in the 1914 Six - takes the win. Flup plays base football that day against the Amicale Sportif Français. It remains 0-0. His track debut is set for November 18.

Ten thousand viewers want to see the pairing race. Deruyter and Thys steal the show, but they mat each other from start to finish. That Egg-Content thoughtfully advance and eventually gain the upper hand, they poorly estimate. So driven are they, so happy to feel the pedals again. In December, in an omnium against Pélissier and Lapize, Philippe gets the win as a gift. Enfant terrible Henri falls and proves unable to ride the final. At 47,200 km/h, the Brussels rider gets the track war record for free.

In 1917, the government gives permission for road races to be resumed. Roubaix is in the front zone, but towards free Tours the old classic can be resumed. The general public has not forgotten the race. Thys, after seven hours and a few race minutes, can leave behind tormentor Godivier. Then Christophe and Mantelet follow. Crupelandt's record time is increased by one minute. Now he has a classic victory, even if it is a lean war edition, in which not all the big names participate.

Three weeks later follows a nice initiative by L'Auto: a new course from picturesque Mont-Saint-Michel to Paris. The morning Manche brings coolness, but the sky that night sucked up too much seawater. Clouds pour gallons of brackish water over the blooming Bocage and Thys waits in Mortagne-au-Perche for the camion with the luggage. Suitcase on the handlebars, he ends up at a sawmill, where changing clothes is no problem. The logger does not recognise Thys, his little son does.

SERIE DE LA GUERRE. — N° 134.   LE NUMERO : 25 CENTIMES   MERCREDI 9 MAI 1917.

SPORTING
EDITIONS SPÉCIALES PENDANT
LA GUERRE

Le départ de Paris - Tours

Cette photo réunit quelques-uns des grands cracks qui participèrent à la course. De gauche à droite : MANTE-LET (arrivé 4°), GODIVIER (2°), VAN DEN HOVE (7°), CRISTOPHE (3°), ALI NEFFATI (9°), NOEL (8°), P. THYS (1°° en 7 heures 14 minutes).

A chair is pushed in, forcing Philippe to spoon out a hefty plate of pot au feu. When he wants to pay for the provided care with a clammy bank note, the woodsman squeezes his shoulder: c'était un plaisir Monsieur Thys et une rencontre à ne jamais oublier. Flup promises to send a clean signed rider's card after and sets off for the nearest station, soon cycling twenty kilometres through the puddles.

The Théâtre du Châtelet premieres Parade, Cocteau's ballet piece set to music by Erik Satie. Picasso designs sets and impractical cubist costumes that make the actors fall over. Lookalikes of soldiers disoriented by blindness and amputated. Shockingly surreal antidote to shrapnel and mustard gas. Cultural resistance to war mode is many times too farfelu to counter the raw cold of the front.

Even the south is in the grip of tristesse on the morning of 4 November. In Italy, the leaves are always allowed to fall a little later in autumn, but now it is damn early winter there. Secluded nervously, Alfonsia Strada - the only woman who could ever ride a classic - stands putting her flannel underwear in order. The donna will later cycle the Giro with the men and make more money from it than the overall winner. Pelissiser keeps the peloton warm with a brisk pace.

▲ Alfonsina Strada.

On the way to Como, a leading group of five hit a two-minute bonus. Juseret and Thys speak up and take turns demarrelling to bring down the local Lucotti-Torricelli coalition. Pélissier also wants to win and brings everyone back each time. With Belloni and Girardengo coming up, they know what to do: spin. The Italian darlings do not return and the joke of the day follows on the cycling track, when the tenors cut each other off along the bottom and top. There are rags to come from that. Thys is in the lead. Pelissiser comes alongside and the Italians wriggle along behind. A good ten metres from the finish, the sprinting cogs carom bottomward. Four pairs of wheels slide across the line.

The judges designate Philippe as the winner. Pélissier, of course, disagrees. Authority figures always work like a rag on a bull with him. Even after complaining, the delegates confirm the result. The uproar subsides when Alfonsina enters the stadium in a final group. An unorthodox second classical win is printed obliquely on the photo, but it counts.

In the run-up to 1918, Thys worries about competitors who are permanently in his way. What are these men eating? Marcel Godivier - admittedly once a great talent - is making an unbridled comeback. He is a tough and wiry sujet with the head of a tango dancer. He will make Flup bite the sand on the cycling tracks several more times. During the charity meeting, to raise money for the monument in honour of Darragnon, it's all over again. Charles Mantelet is the other nefarious one: a war rider pas tout à fait pur sang, who is at the front of everything and will soon not ride a flat prize. At the Parc, the pros ride a Championship of Champions over 100km on 9 May. The child must have a name. There is already so little to do sport-wise. Thys wins, but dismounted on the way to take another bike. Thus Mantelet - who has gone to inform the jury himself - gets the victory as a gift. Jules Messelis growls in West Flemish: that the French always have an explanation and invent new rules on the spot. There are not many moments to retaliate. In Paris-Tours, one week later, Philippe is not even allowed to start. Arriving late due to train delays around the capital, he can't get his bike lead in time. It suits the French so well that one would suspect someone along the track has deliberately left a traffic light on red. Mantelet doesn't mind and once again steals the win.

At Tours-Paris, Thys will probably leave. Flup will take a train earlier this time. The reverse route of the classic is designed to dust off the calendar. Along the front line at Montdidier, the Germans launched an artillery attack the week before. The military leadership promptly withdraws all leave. Consequently, there are only 27 entries. After two nasty tyre breaks and a fall in Orleans, Flup sprints along for the win anyway. Six of them wriggle into Prinsenpark. Pistier Sérès is in sight. The Brussels-based rider takes the lead and is strong. Yet Mantelet comes to harass him again right to the finish. No new lines pop up this time. The jury does what has to be done and the flowers are for the Belgian sergeant.

Meanwhile, Philippe moved his army britches. At Etampes, French and Belgians each have their barracks and airstrips. When ascending and descending, depending on the wind direction, this causes problems of underutilisation. Thys and co. are sent away to a discarded flying strip belonging to the French at Juvisy. The Port-Aviaton is a sunken stretch of land for swimmers and rowers. Good enough for the grotesque Belgian aviators. A stream thwarts the site and regularly floods the area.

Logistically, it is a vast and barely organised encampment. But it is only for a little while. After November 11, no one has to lift a finger. The idle life can begin. In late January 1919, the slow clean-up completed, Flup is fired.

The return to the homeland is not yet going smoothly. Half the world's population wants to take the train home simultaneously and the Spanish flu is hissing through Western Europe like a deadly cobra. Mother is quickly reassured. Hanging around Paris for a while longer won't hurt. There are still some wine bottles hidden in sewers and catacombs for the victory ball.

Contrary to what sports literature already claims, Philippe never hung around in the air as an aviator. When - after the 1922 Tour - he makes his application to the Ministry of Defence to obtain front stripes (war allowance), the answer is negative. As proof, his army record under the number of days of front stay reads: néant. Rail discount or a free bus pass Philippe will never need afterwards.

▲Philippe Thys just won Tours-Paris 1918 in the sprint.

1919

The train

There is snow on the roof of the sports palace when Mayor Mettewie kicks off the Brussels Six Days. During the first night, students force the entrance on Jerusalem Street and, besides the mediocre spectacle, warm themselves up. When Thys and French sprint champion Dupuy win the Brussels Six on the night of 5 April 1919, it is still freezing on the empty benches of the grandstand. The Frenchman with southern accent from Brive-La-Gaillarde, suffered incredible cold.

The pair can keep their bonus round intact until the final day. Aerts-Spiessens and Persijn-Vandevelde complete the podium. These are not exactly the pancakes of the wooden oval. The losers are not at all pleased with the course. Buddies of Thys stopped pedalling behind the leading duo and then deliberately came dribbling into the road. The confederates shrug. Sportingly, the operation differs in nothing from that which Mac Bolle's Flandriens prepare themselves: collude and hold back at crucial moments. The winners tour 4130.125 kilometres. A Tour distance indoors.

Henri Pélissier beats Thys in an equally cold outdoor Paris-Roubaix, flogged by gusts of ice. The face not yet dried, Philippe already pushes away his attendant's towel. A tirade towards journalists kicks in: the French have used linchpin tricks again. First by leaving a train on the level crossing and later by forcing Barthélémy and Pélissier to stick on my wheel. In a rush, Thys makes another complaint about the invisible finish banding. Winner types are bad losers. The first major post-war cycling confrontation is a thriller. Slender brothers Henri and Françis plan to make it a family outing. They go on the attack from afar, despite the hideous weather. When the youngster starts to weaken and has to deal with tyre breaks on top of that, Henri decides to hold back. So Thys comes to the front on stocking feet and immediately sees that Françis has been betrayed by his youthful hubris. Flup eliminates him immediately, but that is not counting on Bartélémy, who can still keep up with the tenors, who are slightly slowing down. The three of them go swiftly towards Roubaix, until in the Lille suburb of Lesquin a train blocks the level crossing. Pélissier is nervous. Riders are reported a short distance away. Henri takes flight by surprise; opens the door of a carriage and hoists his bike inside. The two others hesitate. Until, under the train carriage, they see a pair of tall socks riding away. They react late and it takes forces to reconnect. The unforeseen epilogue kills Thys. In a fair final, he could never lose on the track. Were they allowed to ignore a level crossing back then? Or is a stationary train heir power? Paris-Robaais calls L' Enfer du Nord after that bad edition. The bombs caused so much destruction that out of 40 follow cars, five made it to the finish. The riders do better: 25 suckers complete the ride. Road conditions and the limited condition of the peloton reduce the race speed sharply everywhere.

By today's standards, the 1919 Tour would never have taken place; conditions just a little more awkward than the two centimetres of snow somewhere between Kuurne and Brussels. Above the Loire, there are virtually no more continuous road links. Of the eight million active French men who were to become soldiers, more than six million were dead or wounded. They died at the rate of a thousand a day. Every time the earth turned shamefully away to the moon, another two thousand were wounded. Day by day, for four years. An entire generation disappears.

Like the human bodies, the topinambour fields that saved France from starvation are exhausted and emptied. There is insufficient food and not even bedding available. Rubber to make bicycle tyres is barely available. Remaining ones are sold at the price of gold bars. Any innkeeper, who can display a beautiful piece of meat under his inviting white towel, turns out to be an impostor, charging unreal cash. The wildlife population has been decimated. Dogs and cats simmer in the stews, even among distinguished citizens. Of the original fleet of 66,000 vehicles for the Grande Guerre, few usable ones remain and there is hardly any petrol. Driving an endurance race in these conditions seems impossible.

For four years, all energy and money went to the front line. The Circuit des Champs de Bataille (Tour of the Battlefields) run during May as a tribute to the fallen proves that. At no point is it a regular road race. The immense plod through mud and debris, feels like an obstacle course through minefields and trenches. It looks like a poorly

timed mountain bike ride avant la lettre. Streets are smashed by the Great War, landscapes ripped open into huge craters that still smell of solfer. Riders crawl on twisted signposts at dusk; to look for the name of the town where they are then long no longer expected. If that was even invented, at least they rode back home, away from this macabre spectacle. Nobody dared to organise the race afterwards, so much stain was left on the awful 1919 edition.

The situation did not improve at the beginning of July. But Desgrange must and will have his race, against all advice and friendly persuasion. Even the bike manufacturers cannot help him. Their market has collapsed, the factories partly dismantled. Though bad guys whisper that their carriage manufactures did make money for the army. Brands that fiercely competed with each other before WWI are now forging an alliance to force the pros to pay hefty wages. With the creation of La Sportive as the umbrella payment agency, the manufacturers are making everyone pay big bucks in the name of rebuilding the country and cycling. The monopoly hits the riders fiercely.

Iron, steel? There is no bar in stock. With the message that they can kiss both hands because the constructors are still providing them with enough material, the riders should be more than satisfied. That the Tour will benefit all in all is the clincher with which La Sportive gets the Tour boss on its side. Desgrange lives in a love-hate relationship with the riders' livelihoods. Indeed, extreme brand interests have permanently undermined his event.

That everyone will now act on their own more than ever makes the fight more open and the founder objective ally of the consortium. Still, there are fears that the Pélis-siers will run amok and threaten general rioting. This must be avoided at all costs. Their agreement is more than desirable. To everyone's surprise, they smoothly agree to La Sportive's policy. Knowing the clan, that could also be pure hubris. The day after, they make fools of everyone and go to independent constructor Louvet. He cannot really offer them any significant extras, but the brothers prefer adventure to uniformity. That's just how they were put together. In 1921 - by now with La Sportive anyway - they do even more farsighted, by cancelling their contract and racing as individuals.

1919

Troubles in Le Havre

P hilippe mumbles inside weary evangelical words. It is only a rehearsal text. That steenezel of a Pélissier, wait until I get to speak to him: fetes Thys. Do they at La Sportive really think we're going to plough 5000 kilometres across France with a hungry belly full of turnips and nothing on our bill: keutes Flup some more. There is little reaction. In the ears of friends like Lapize, Faber, Engel and Petit-Breton, it would have sounded different. However, they had remained at the front for good.

Most blamed their deaths on hubris. They were framed by the French government and thrown into the fray to fulfil a role pattern. Thys is talking today to a generation that sees in the prize harvest and publicity a stepping stone to better times. The Brussels man makes his account and decides against the terms of La Sportive and Desgrange not to perform. Watch out, because I'm quitting in the first Tour stage: he throws the Peugeot bosses off. These wave away the threat.

Staying away as an outgoing winner is not an option. The French masters will never put up with that. They can deny him equipment and claim breach of contract. Philippe has no option. He has to start, but he has a plan in his backpack. The general mood is apparently not yet grey enough: all the first category riders are at the start in a sallow grey mouse jersey. A small centre band - white for Thys - on the sleeve should make them individually identifiable. Exuberant colours are still inappropriate. The Buyze brothers may wear the blue of Bianchi. Louvet's racing stable will bring its own team to the start. JB is the only major French constructor to reject the coalition and dip its own green beans. Exactly 66 riders descended on Paris: a setback. Niséret, Kopp and Devilly cancelled at the last minute. Thys is already starting to rallied as he collects his bib number. With "13" he does not want to start under any circumstances. Lambot has no problem changing his number 14. Desgrange knows it is best not to give the former winner too much food for grumbles and agrees.

The Germans sign the Treaty of Versailles. So on Saturday, one war is already over in time and definitively, before the next one can erupt on Sunday. Between the Parc des Princes and the official start in Argenteuil, pledge Francis Pélissier breaks a wheel. If Paris is full of craters, what will it look like outside the city gates? Henri's younger brother needs two hours to recover and get out of the city. He would have been better off staying in Paris, as the ride to Le Havre is a stumble of tumbles, popping tyres and mechanic incidents.

The main roads have not improved after a drought. Dust clouds obstruct visibility and every so often, load carts of roadworkers are in the way. 41 push-throughs reach the coast. Thys has been having stomach problems all day. Within sight of the ocean, he steers into a ditch and bites into the chalky dust. The significant incident takes place three kilometres from the finish line, in the coastal town of Sainte-Adresse, on Belgian soil, where the government had been in exile during WWI. Flup straightens up and gives up.

Thys sees Le Havre from the sloping sand dune. He has only a scraped knee. But then, as in a predictable gangster film, suddenly, out of nowhere, a big car comes driving onto the scene. Philippe puts his bike in the back seat and gets in. If there is no statement behind that, what is? As if they were part of the advertising caravan - which would not appear until 1930 - the company rides into the port city on Tour roads. Magical realism? The Belgian just barely throws out signed shots. Monsieur Henri cannot believe his eyes. Does this sakkerse This dare leave his Tour already on the first day and in such a way? It is unacceptable for someone who, as a central figure, had to colour the restart of the event. The director is so angry that he did award winner Rossius the stage win, but then foisted half an hour of penalty time on him. The Walloon gave Philippe a drink can along the way. Rossius has the monstrous misfortune to happen to be in the draft of the Tour boss's furious verbiage. Anybody could have been given a bus. Several if need be, but Thys under no circumstances. Penalty time makes Henri Pélissier the first leader and that is no obstacle for the front page of L' Auto.

'Flup' did not dare remove his bike from the back seat and quietly drove on. In the meantime, Flup has already fled France. Desgrange sends him another fine of 50 francs: for unauthorised provisioning. Out of sorts, he considers foisting another fine on Thys, for the inevitable crossing of the Greenwich meridian at the same Veulletes-sur-Mer.

Philippe was picked up at Le Havre by an attendant, who did manage to predict particularly well where to pick up the fallen champion.... Once home and out of the eye of the storm, he need not have worried. In the Tour meetings afterwards, on the slopes of the Borinage, he gets to help pick up money and even bring brother Guillaume to the starting line.

Desgrange, for his part, has still not recovered. Worse than accusing the Brussels man of premeditation, he distils a story that is many times more painful for an athlete. Thys fell over and got out to hide his poor condition, as he had left with a lot of excess weight, unworthy of a top athlete: writes L' Auto on a blue Monday.

Later that year, the editor-in-chief will once again bring out his sharpened pen and jeeringly refer to Flup as: petit-bourgeois, complètement perdu pour le sport cycliste. According to that theory, no one needs to engage in the true debate: about La Sportive's motives and L'Auto's erroneous organisational assessment. Anyone who still wins a six-day race in April, co-decides the final of Paris-Roubaix and continues to ride weekly meetings cannot possibly have got off the train in Paris as a pot-bellied fatty. All the more so because Flup is so fond of his body culture and was still whizzing through Orleans in Bordeaux-Paris in a favourable position. After an unfortunate fall, he sets off in hot pursuit and gets appreciations in the newspapers for it.

Confronted with the myth of obesity, Thys replies: that in 1919, there were no fat people and that even the Germans depicted in war propaganda with round bellies left our lands as skinny skinnies. He adds delicately: that given the quality of food and subsoil that year, everyone had the right to get sick and fall over.

▲ Firmin Lambot becomes the third Belgian ever to win the Tour de France.

France will no longer enjoy its 1919 Tour de France. Desgrange promises improvement in the more intact south of the country, but the bulk of the riders fail to reach their destination. At the end of the miserable Tour, the boss writes in a moment of eccentric otherworldliness : "J'ai ramené mes onze poilus: je peux dire que ce sont de fiers lapins." ("I've brought home my eleven plucked chickens: I can tell they're proud rabbits.")

1919
Gold or yellow?

A long the Atlantic coast, honourable Pélissiers are stringing together stage wins. Henri, a classy but neurotic flayer, easily goes through the roof after success. Today, one would prescribe that gentleman a big box of rilatine at the first doctor's visit. Once in the winning mood, the slender Frenchman always has a divinely self-assured side. The thoroughbred often calls his Belgian competitors vulgar work-horses.

When La Ficelle makes a puddle at a sadly dripping forest edge and calmly takes off a rain vest, the workhorses collectively stampede. The thoroughbred solo manages to make up some of his 20-minute deficit. But that effort is not sustainable even for a Pélissier. Brother and Barthélémy - who deliberately go puncturing in the gravier to be allowed to wait - join the chase. The Tour boss sees it as forbidden collective action and threatens exclusion.

Henri suddenly steps off and rants that they can hear it all the way to the parental dairy farm in the XVI arrondissement: one question Mr director, do they ride up front individually? Why don't you go and have a look there ...Pélissier has a point. The rules are not always clear, but now the man applying them is cheating. To everyone's surprise, the trio gets back on their bikes to ride out. Better bullying is in the making. Why would Henri give up in this forgotten and deserted village, totally out of sight?

The brothers get newspaper forum to accuse Desgrange of bias. On nous veut du mal: let them blockletter. The morning after the rest day looks dead normal. The Pélissiers have a solemn breakfast, calm as can be, they listen to suggestive questions and give objective answers. Then they re-enter their room and crawl into bed. Desgrange refuses to knock on the door as the Tour prepares to get under way. It is the beginning of a long saga. Things never actually work out between Henri and Henri again. Desgrange later writes, after yet another clash with the hothead, that the elder Pélissier has l' inextricablenervosité de jolie femme. Alevoine has to save the French in the remaining rides towards the midi. At the Spanish border, they are still with 17. After the Alps, they are still with 11. The Tour is on haircuts. Something has to be invented and the boss knocks on leader Christophe's door with a yellow jersey. The ever-cooperative Eugène doesn't like wearing the gaudy thing and being recognisable to everyone all day.

But Monsieur le Directeur can convince, and if that fails, play dictator. So it happens that someone has to bet the next morning amid roaring laughter from spectators and riders. Christophe, le canari, gets used to his plumage and the round has a news event. The duts will not make it to Paris in his yellow feathers because, again, Desgrange, wants to treat the peloton to 100 kilometres of stones from the north if necessary. A side note. In Raimes, Christophe breaks his fork yet again, this time with a clear prospect of overall victory.

The Tour boss gives and takes. Lambot from Florennes walks away with the overall win. He earns 6,000 francs. That's not much for so much sacrifice and a lot of personal expenses. Thys forces the final word on the yellow jersey scoop. He testified to a French journalist that Desgrange had wanted to score twice with the same idea. Philippe is also said to have been approached in the 1913 or 14 round to ride in a flashy leader's jersey. By whom he leaves a little confused, but does recall winking that it took so much persuasion that finals money was offered. The then class leader did not consider yellow recognisability an advantage either. Nevertheless, at the hands of either the Tour boss or Baugé, he puts on une tunique dorée. The jersey gets so dirty and soiled along the way that it is permanently left in a laundry basket at the next stop. Flup also remembers: that the right size was found in a shop in Geneva, but that the fastening at the top was too tight and was made into a kind of décolleté de grande dame with scissors.

We can quickly agree on gold or yellow. Yellow in the Middle Ages was a cheap colour without standing, easy to make unlike noble red and blue. After brushing, yellow inexplicably turns brown quickly. Van Gogh's flower fields know all about it. Worn rags without fresh perspective have become it through oxidation years. Gold is more solid. Something that wants to shine must contain gold thread. The leader's jerseys in the tours of Switzerland and formerly Spain, were officially gold, not mean yellow. If there was a leader's suit before World War I, Desgrange may have had little to do with it. The obvious link to the paper colour on which the organising newspaper is printed has been proven only for the pink of the Gazzetta dello Sport.

The Tour boss is not a man of distinction and colour. He prefers everyone to start in the same jersey, with the same bike, the same number of spare tyres and the same water flow for the road. All the same and the struggling athlete will make the difference. Desgrange's thoughts on yellow in 1919 may have been purely motivated by the seriousness of the situation and the need to get out of the crisis. The archives of L'Auto are lost during WWII and no newspaper mentions the unique leader's jersey at the time of Thys. Nevertheless, the three-time winner is known for his seriousness and gives many details, but also false and contradictory indications. With types who always want to win, one has to be careful. If need be, they also want to wear the only first yellow jersey. In 1920, it officially reads, something went wrong when the jerseys were ordered and made. Leader Philippe gets his first yellow only in Nice as a result.

Does he insist on handing over the jersey in his second hometown? In any case, he gets only a chemise Lacoste. The summer pullover must serve as a stopgap. Actual tights are still not available after ride nine. That says a lot about the way Desgrange is more likely not to care than to care. A necessary novelty in 1919, the jersey is hardly a focus of attention one year later. Nobody bothers to have the status symbol readily available. This is not how we know the Tour management, because if necessary they will have a detail brought over by plane if necessary.

Is Thys mistaken when he talks about buying in Geneva? Is Nice the place of the shopping trip? Or did he indeed wear a gold jersey in 1913 or 14, but rather as a publicity stunt, Roman Emperor Cipollini way ahead? Thys was obviously leading the standings at the time, but perhaps one has nothing to do with the other. No one can figure out the exact facts yet. Or did Thys have bon in it to prank the press, which effectively writes anything if it smells like a scoop? Baugé in particular is in a yellow period in those days. It is he, who paints Peugeot's racing bikes yellow and has a wide yellow band embroidered into the dull blue jerseys, who is behind the facts? The guru is Desgrange's daily listening ear and may offer advice. If anyone gets something sold to management, it is Baugé. Is he wearing out his own dream?

Is making the Peugeot leader stroll on a yellow bike in a yellow jersey his childlike triumph? The introduction of yellow alongside classic blue in the Peugeot logo, has everything to do with the drive for visibility. For a company that wants to be recognisable on the Tour roads, colour is primordial. For a sports director always hot behind the group in dusty conditions, recognisability is equally important.

Advertising techniques have always captivated the lion mark and yellow and red have always fought robberies as cut attention colours, right down to the poles of our traffic lights. The security world has since settled the matter, giving yellow-black precedence over red-white. Again, wasn't it Peugeot that struggled with that colour dilemma back in the 1930s? They temporarily replaced yellow jersey wool with red. When black-and-white images brought the first live television broadcasts into living rooms, Peugeot was once again the first to jump out of the picture with the legendary checkerboard jersey.

Thys would win the stage to Metz in 1920, where the true jersey was finally ready. Consequently, the three-time Tour winner has only ridden with an official yellow jersey for two days: to Dunkirk and to Paris, in 1920. A meagre harvest for someone who has been in the lead so many times. It is manly if he wanted to add another forgotten stage.

PHILIPPE THYS

Vainqueur du troisième tour de France cycliste

1920

Landru

....

Quirky Philippe will return to the Tour in 1920 mainly to give everyone a licking. Desgrange is the first to know of these plans. Thys writes him a curt letter in the winter of 1920, after the new allegations in L'Auto. The prediction going to Paris under cover is prophetically clear.

The Tour boss remains enough of a sportsman to rehabilitate and appreciate the Brussels man; as long as it doesn't have to be in public. The Belgians overwhelmed his lap emphatically enough. Permissive and flexible, Desgrange will never again become. These notions were advised against him throughout his youth. He belongs to the generation that offers its back to be caned, loyal to authority figures. Authority must be enforced and is the only lifeline society can cling to. Historians argue that stubborn customs from a staid era are only discarded after WWI, and then the 20th century begins. Arriving at insights does not necessarily mesh with flexibility and willingness to change. The half aristocrat leading the Tour has his upbringing against him.

Serial killer Henri-Désiré Landru has now been caught. Le barbu will pay like no other for murdering, dismembering and roasting as many as 10 women. The guillotine is unpacked, sharpened and greased. The state system still exudes power. But a new order is in the making. Travaillist and nationalist ideas are pep talks. Seed for a different society has been strewn, it is germinating and weeding is a hopeless task. Mussolini's Camicie Nere are marching on Rome as Flup gives shape to his word and sets out from Milan to take the first hurdle to the predicted resurrection.

◀ Philippe Thys wins a stage in the 1920 Tour de France.

Things stupidly go wrong that March 25 in faraway Italy. At an idiotic wooden bridge on a cramped mountain path, things poach and guide his shoulder to the cornerstone of a wall over a ruscello. Pats. The key bone gives way and Thys stumbles over the first stepping stone to his third Tour victory. Forfait for Roubaix and Tours.

A stroke of luck. The Tour is still a long way off. Philippe walks himself silly in April to stay in shape. In Bordeaux-Paris, he makes it to the control of Amboise. At the foot of the picturesque castle on the Loire, there are 363 kilometres on the counter. Together with De-jonghe, he steps off the course, straight into a restaurant. The Tour of Belgium is not on the programme. Philippe does come to the start in Tervuren, to wish his brother luck and then cycle towards Namur himself. He wants to do lots and long practice days and be good in Paris-Brussels.

When the capital classic is neutralised for 15 minutes at the Agimont border crossing, Flup is still fresh and fit. Taking the hills poses no problem at all. In Namur, the group breaks and on the Tombeek mountain - where Charles V hands out silver coins every year - there are still six of them. Mottiat is unlucky, but gets back between the cars at lightning speed. He is a candidate winner. De Waal can't put it away. Pélissier does. Henri puts himself in the right rear wheel and does not let go of that position. In the sports palace, the Frenchman shows metier. Mottiat feels it won't work out and grabs his attacker by the arm to still arrive first, more a reflex than malice. Vermandel runs in third. Then comes Thys, who takes a passing exam.

Mottiat may take revenge in the Tour's opening stage from Paris to Le Havre. He is faster in the sprint than companions Rossius, Thys, Goethals and Masson. Flup is up to the mark and puts other competitors there at 15 minutes already. To complete the psychological joust, he wins the mass sprint in Cherbourg the following day. That was not initially the plan, until arrogant Henri proclaims that it is best to look for a beautiful mademoiselle in the harbour to laud him. Without exceptional female beauty, he will not come to the stage. Thys usually lets the braggart rant, but occasionally it gets too powerful for him. The haughty fool needs a lesson from time to time.

▲ Thys at the head of Mont Angel, followed by Aymo.

▲ Scieur followed by Masson at the summit of the Toumalet.

▲ Thys wins the hilly sprint in Nice.

▲ Thys passes must dodge a careless spectator at the Praches checkpoint during the seventh stage to Perpignan.

▲ Eugène Christophe refreshes, surrounded by curious onlookers.

On stage three from Cherbourg to Brest, Pélissier stands his ground and in turn wins the sprint ahead of Masson, Christophe and Thys. Philippe, however, is supreme. He feels he can ride them all off. The day after in the stage from Brest to Sables d'Olonne, Pélissier challenges again. Philippe calmly stays in his tracks. Fil de fer has stung considerably this year. But he also rides supreme and really kicks in the butter. Giving the ever confident Henri a spanking in Olonne would be fun. The linkeball plays it too smart in the sprint. Philippe has to hit the brakes and comes up short to attack the Frenchman. He cannot afford to take risks. After all, the Tour is not a game.

In the fifth stage, it is Lambot's turn. He wins the sprint ahead of Thys and the big group. Philippe has everyone sitting like gnomes in the pocket of his race jersey. No one can hurt him. Whether he will be able to ride away from his opponents? It would be blissful to know, but not yet on the cards. Patience is a virtue. The first five stages end in a mass sprint. Desgrange detests that. He wants to see the riders crouch individually. Was it a fable that Henri's dream was a Tour in which only one rider would reach the finishing line? Pélissier, honourable bad character hors catégorie, has already dropped out of the Tour after being fined for throwing away a broken tube. In doing so, he is once again highlighting the director's inhuman side. Thys did not wait a year earlier for a trivial tube incident to step out of the insubstantial authority scene. He does not run amok in public like Pélissier. Much more subtly, however, he does just the same.

A visit to good friend Christophe, who has been battling a kidney infection for days, is reasonable. The veteran cannot keep the bed at night from the pain. Cri-cri is exhausted and capitulates in the Pyrenees, where Lambot unpacks again in the sixth stage from Bayonne to Luchon. The Walloon's changing climbing rite is hard to follow. He is the mountain king of his time, descending like a stone in the process. Firmin has lost a lot of time in the early stages. He is an hour behind and is no longer a threat. Philippe comes down cautiously and arrives second at two minutes and a bit. Heusghem, Scieur and Masson do not approach and the French do not feature in the piece.

Heading towards Perpignan, they are up by five. Now Rossius gets to win the sprint, ahead of Thys, Scieur, Lambot et les autres. Masson stays behind, until it turns out that he has been sent the wrong way by a commissioner and is touring villages where

◀ A lone Philippe Thys while climbing a Pyrenean col.

he does not need to be. Emile regains that lost hour. Desgrange has evidence that Thys is donating rides away in exchange for tranquillity and takes the Belgian to task heavily. Philippe admits to having been quite impressed: I was called to the post office, which served as the Tour boss' office and where no conversation was possible with the exited Desgrange, only listening duty. He was played over his head and made it clear that in sport the best must always win and the opposite is unsportsmanlike. More serious was his threat to exclude me based on regulations. If he started talking about regulations, you had better pay attention. Finally, dixit Thys followed with the classically correct courtesy formula: You can go Sir and don't ignore the verwitting or I will kick you out of my course. Philippe took the safe course and saw suits of lire pierced through his nose. Tant pis. The Italians rarely come to the Tour in top form, but are keen to win a stage. To make that happen, they rely on wild benefactors. These offer exuberant sums, sometimes embarrassingly high to accept without pudeur.

On the eighth stage from Perpignan to Aix-en-Provence, the Heusghem brothers come out of their hole. They set up an offensive together. Thys does not enter the duel. He will not let the blood tie crush him. The elder Louis is allowed to ride off. Hector is much shorter in the rankings.

With the line of the ninth stage in Nice, the weighing of gifts is briefly interrupted. Lambot wants to get away, but Thys goes after him with Scieur, leaving both friends behind on the descent to Menton. Vandaele does another brilliant remount, but folds in the finale. The stage ends on the velodrome for the first time. Under the concrete entrance arch of the Chemin de la Madeleine, Flup looks back once more pro forma and then dashes triumphantly onto the piste. Hector gets half an hour on his trousers and is now second in the standings an hour behind Thys. Firmin Lambot follows in third 20 minutes further away. The morning papers are formal: Thys, vainqueur, compte une heure d'avance sur ses adversaires.

Desgrange emerges on the rest day with a temporary chemise jaune. The real leader's jerseys are not delivered and the Tour boss hides that flaw in the organisation, insisting that no one deserves the jersey. The 1920 lap cannot captivate and is locked. Thys reigns supreme. Nobody can do anything in return and every few days, whenever and wherever he wants, Philippe puts everyone to shame. A dry reserved effort produces a little extra lead each time.

The agony of his opponents is not over. A lead sun travels with them on their tour of France. The man in the greatest forme suffers the least. Hector wins the stage from Nice to Grenoble, but yellow is the dominant colour poking into his back. Maybe they can give Philippe another hard time in the next stage, over the Galibier, to Gex?

Scieur, Lambot and the Heusghem brothers get a turn or two ahead. It becomes several minutes after the summit. Thys gives free rein. They can fight it out among themselves, while he will slalom downhill at his leisure. Without nervous hustlers around, this works best and it also remains to watch out for pits and goats. Scieur glows in the valley. The stage winner and his companions receive no congratulations from the Tour boss, only a distant rebuke. They failed to really attack Thys.

In stage 12 from Gex to Strasbourg, the same names seize command. Philippe prepares for a nippy sprint on the cycling track. There may be some fun moments for him after all. The speedy Rossius does threaten, but comes up short. Winning with telling ease, will earn Thys a street name (now cycling route) to the old Saint Anne maternity hospital.

How supreme can you be without permanently upsetting everyone. It is an art of living that few athletes have mastered. Without flinching, the yellow man-to-be once again wins the group sprint in Metz. That is how tired all his opponents are and that is how closely Desgrange continues to watch the sporting outcome of each ride. Thys wants to share, but points in the direction of the chief marshal every time.

▲ Thys wins the sprint of the sprinting peloton in Strasbourg.

In the penultimate stage from Metz to Dunkirk, overconfident Philippe did not count on a remount from Nordist Goethals, though tipped for the ride to his home beach. Or are they fooling the Tour boss professionally that day? Goethals wins in front of his own people. Did Philippe get dough? Even if Desgrange already suspected, it was now too late to punish the Belgian and above all, contest the sincerity of a scarce French stage win.

Enough is enough. L' Auto no longer achieves circulation and the Tour boss decides to quietly let his round die out. Can the final chord in Paris still provide a surprise winner? Rossius - remembering Strasbourg - takes on Thys in front of packed grandstands in Paris. The dehumanisation of the final winner is thus halted just in time. The best has won: with almost an hour's bonus on Heusghem. Even if the winner achieves one of the lowest averages ever, the press writes about a great champion: un valleureux who brushes aside Petit-Breton's record with a snap of his fingers. Four stage wins, co-leading the second day and no daily classification outside the top five. It may suffice. But some Parisian newspapers are still talking about: Thys roi des veinards. His tacky riding does not please the old cycling world. Philippe no longer cares. Or does it affect him inside anyway?

At the classic straight interview after his third overall victory, Thys will be very clear on the mic about the Tour and his boss. In front of a well-filled Parc, he will bravely take advantage of the cutting sound reinforcement to announce: that if Desgrange does nothing about his inhuman regulations, he will not return.

▲ In Nice, Thys wins ahead of Heusghem. He wins four stages in this Tour de France, it could even have been 11....

▲ In Briançon beat Thys Sellier by a wheel length.

▲ Rossius won the sprint of the final stage in Paris, followed by Philippe Thys by a bike length.

The Belgians returned no fewer than 11 of 15 rides in 1920 and occupied seven top places in the reckoning. The French are ridiculed. Barthélemy does not dare give up despite a broken shoulder and an inflamed eye. He follows in eighth place, at almost six hours.

If my third victory brought me closer to super champion status, it was more in Paris and France than in Belgium, the man from Brussels will often say. It could hardly be otherwise. Thys will always respect Anderlecht as his home, but he is not planted in the clay like the sons of Flemish farmers in the middle of their village yard. Flup is an urbanite who, from an early age, surfs away along the murky Senne without homesickness, always searching and groping for better surroundings and practice prowess. Then you cannot bind ardent local supporters and free up particularist court writers at the newspaper.

That Philippe's successes remain emotionally untranslated in the newspapers and do not evoke enough enthusiasm and ecstasy among the people is the logical consequence of his being too much of a life and wheel. An exuberant celebration in Brussels is du déja vu. In the home community, they find something to do with that. The municipal sports stadium and park - in use since 1917 - are finally finished. As the apotheosis of a three-day party with sports competitions, gymnastics exhibitions and music, the Tour winner will drop by in the late afternoon. Nonkel Joseph, party director at the Sporting, has everything pitch-perfectly scheduled. Prince Leopold

▲ Thys at the head of the chasing group in the final stage to Paris.

▲ Rossius won the sprint of the final stage in Paris, followed by Philippe Thys by a bike length.

▲ Thys at the head of the pack ahead of Léon Scieur, during the climb of van Poix in the final stage to Paris.

▲ Philippe Thys at the arrival of the 1920 Tour de France.

presses Thys' hand. The new purple-and-white stand flawlessly handles the pressure of a first standing ovation.

Henry George wins gold in the 50 kilometres a few days later, in front of empty stands, at the City Garden cycling track. The people of Antwerp prefer to party downtown. Ommeganckweek does not give way to the drawn-out Olympics. Thys, for his part, is still lauded by Brussels Sportive with a sculpture by de Zoete and a long list of equally long-winded accolades. Afterwards, he and Van Hevel cannot be in Italy soon enough. Letting off steam and riding Lombardy in November. Pushing and pulling clouded the atmosphere in the boot. Mussolini's militias prey on northern villages. Civil war looms and then staying in Paris is the better idea. Flup rides on All Saints Day in Grenelle and later in Tours. The Giro di Lombardia, where they would have loved to see him back, will be for next year.

74. Anderlecht l'Inauguration du Stade.
S.R. Le Prince Léopold félicite Ph. Thys le
vainqueur du Tour de France ayc. 1920. J.R.B.

PRIJS : Fr. 0.60

BEHEER
N OPSTELRAAD

Werkplaatsenstraat, 3
BRUSSEL

Telefoon
BRUSSEL 149.41

GEILLUSTREERDE SPORTWERELD

ABONNEMENTEN
BELGIE:
3 maand . . . fr. 6
6 — . . . — 12
12 — . . . — 18
FRANKRIJK:
3 maand . . . fr. 6
6 — . . . — 12
12 — . . . — 24
HOLLAND:
3 maand . . . gul. 4
6 — . . . — 6
12 — . . . — 8
Men schrijft in op alle Po

EERSTE JAAR -- N° 9 === VERSCHIJNT OM DE 10 DAGEN === 28ste MEI 1921

BORDEAUX-PARIJS

De overwinnaar Eugeen Christophe, gekiekt na het afstappen.   In medaljon, Filiep Thys, de zedelijke overwinnaar.

1921

Philippe then and now

· ·

Thys with his teammates from Brussels Sportif.

One year is not the other. Philippe of today also had to sweat it out. Soon speculations then surface, about devolution and too little winter will. Indeed, it often has to do with starting later, fulfilling a bit more commitments or simply enjoying a unique win streak. The cycling puzzle law is implacable: those who start less strengthened cannot find the right piece of the puzzle card from the start and then never get the story laid perfectly. So non-existent is the chance that bad luck will come to disturb a rider on the move, the more obvious an accident never comes alone when things are a little less smooth.

Philippe fared identically from then on. The Easter derby (Paris-Roubaix long held on Easter Sunday) 1921 comes early, in clear skies and wind chill around freezing. Everything runs on wheels until den berg van Doullens. Today, that hump is a forgotten depression in the landscape. In later years, the classic will have to lose distance and look for cobbles to keep its name alive. The route will be deflected towards Cambrai. Thys is punctured on the false flat from Beauval and is unable to connect with the big guns along the long line of trees to the summit of Doullens. Almost at the top, the trees stop and a fan-like plateau takes over. The cue for the Pélissiers to give extra throttle. Only Scieur and Vermandel cramp up. Until Henri places the decisive tease in Hem, where by then there is no chunky tarmac next to the cobbles. Francis

◀ Eugène Christophe wins Bordeaux-Paris,

puts himself in the wheels. The sweet brothers become one and two in the new Stade Dubrulle. Thys is left with a portion of doubt and just barely fails to get off. Girardengo, Brunero, Azzini and others give him the same unpleasant feeling one week later. In Conference resort Sanremo, Flup rewinds the film of the ride in his hotel room. Scratching on the Turchino, capitulating along the coast when Girardengo evaporates and on the Capi seeing the lidded eldest of the Pélissiers still riding away from him. There is no power and punch available to make the course with him. Losing 17 minutes is far too much. It is barren. A rider knows from himself whether a tenth place in the spring is a matter of basic fitness or extra sharpening.

Milan-Turin is no different: constantly raking to avoid going off. Can it get any better? In Bordeaux-Paris, Thys should be able to give a sign of life. The condition is better. Set off in pouring rain, the discouraged little pack can only cover a coat for the first time by morning. The backs of Pélissier, Mottiat, Christophe, Rossius, Deman and Heusghem push ahead of Flup. By Angerville, they have rounded 500km. When the Chartreuse is gently pushed under the wet wheels, Christophe is overwhelmingly the best. Alavoine and Thys hang on to their wagons.

Deman and Heusghem set a bad example and boarded the train in Dourdan that brought the pigeons. All the toppers secretly disappear from the drowned course. Philippe would do the same in normal circumstances. Now he has to bite through to know where things stand. When Christophe punctures, Thys smells his chance. Now he will quickly feel what's left in his tank. Alavoine can't keep up. The lead is increasing. He is out of sight: a boost in this winding castle scenery. It looks promising. Until, on a faint descent, there is a sleeve-frosting incident with pacesetter Anseeuw. They overcorrect, lose their balance and collide hard with the road surface. At that point, the distance race is contested with live pacers: pedalling riders who have mercenary status and keep the enrolled leader out of the wind and are allowed to pick up anywhere.

The enlisted pistier and brother-in-law of the Buysse brothers really has the heart of it. If the arm cannot go higher than thigh height and pain shoots up the neck, there is no need to hesitate. Fortunately, the key bone does not play up to that extent. Anseeuw is now pulling even harder, but to no avail. Christophe smells a win. After Alavoine, the unlucky rider crosses the line in third place. The last sixty kilometres were unusually painful. At 10pm, Paul Coppens follows, four hours after the brave winner and out of time.

▲ In 1921, Léon Scieur cycled his way into Tour history.

At a Paris hospital, the Brussels man knows by then what time it is. A collarbone is broken after all. Still making it to the Tour is impossible. Thys will fake it: start knowing it is a measure of nothing. He won't be able to cycle aptly in June. The Belgian Championship on the twisty L'Argentine circuit - after the small river - in La Hulpe is an irritating race. Turning 35 laps does not suit Thys and falling would spoil everything. He forfeits. Real stage racers have an unquenchable reflex to eliminate any risk in view of that one race. It is patently Tour-autism.

Playing poker with bad cards and hoping the flat entry rides go quietly is all Philippe can do. It takes him a lot of effort to believe in that. Barely out of Paris, Thys starts accelerating. Once again the reflex of the round man: sow doubt against his better judgment. When Masson opens the real debates in Dieppe, he ticks off all those playing hide-and-seek mercilessly. It will soon be over when the familiar dusty bric-à-brac roads come to Le Havre.

For Mottiat, those shifting gravel tracks are the signal for the final. The outgoing winner is not good enough and, on top of that, far too cautious. Thys is cramped on his bike, even more lumpy and anxious than usual. The harbour clock ticks away 45 minutes. Flup grabs past the finish line to the wooden barrier. Even before anyone has had a chance to ask anything, he says coolly: we're going home. It will be an open round, completely different from 1920. Rossius, Masson and Heusghem also have to give up quickly. Scieur unexpectedly gets the lead. The bonk from Florennes does not have his looks with him and did not learn to cycle until adulthood. With the gabarit of a forester, shovels of hands and a rough head, it is difficult to exude ingenuity and savoir vivre. However, Scieur beside the bike is a considerate man with great literary hunger and a French accent that the Academie Française cannot improve on him. At the head of the cultured family, which buys a large Ardennes village house with garage workshop at the end of the war, is a confident madam of a pound more. Gently she figures right behind her husband-driver. Exceptional gifts Leon does not have. Heusghem is more powerful, Lambot - who made him a pro rider - the better climber, Thys more flyer. But Scieur never gives up, always stays near them, in all areas the head stronger than the legs. He and Thys are buddies. The man from Brussels regularly descends to the Famenne, looking for suitable training grounds. At the Scieur family's place, there is always a board and a bed ready. Flup even has his domicile there for a while. Lambot - the other villagois of little Florennes - fled to Flanders after stopping over in Charleroi. He too will have a safe refuge from the Antwerp flying bombs during WWII at the hospitable Leon.

With Scieur in yellow and small time gaps, many rivals keep faith on the overall victory cool. In Long Leon, no one sees a Tour winner. In Anderlecht, though, people are keeping their fingers crossed for a good friend. On the way to Nice, Scieur gives his nearest rival Heusghem an extra tap. The latter then hopes for a turnaround in the Alps, but does not come any closer. Even for the good-hearted Ardennes rider, the pen trip to Dunkirk almost ends in failure. To avoid a penalty, Scieur straps a broken wheel on his back. He has to be able to show it at the finish. On arrival, the wheel axle sticks into the tanned back flesh like a skewer. The unique comb wheel Tour tattoo remains lifelong evidence of his perseverance. With a jubilant Parc ahead, the wound feels no worse than a big mosquito bite. The garagist makes it.

For Thys, there is nothing left but to build up skilfully, to unpack once more in the autumn. The richly endowed newcomer Paris-Lyon is a clean opportunity. In the Parisian district of Villejuif, 15 duos start at the beginning of September and are allowed to ride their course free and clear. At the finish, the times of the teammates are added up. It is something different. It's right up Thys' street, who starts with Rossius.

▲ Jacquinot, Bellanger, Thys, Rossius and Vermandel open the Paris-Lyon debates.

▲ In Chalon-sur-Saone, Thys leaves in the lead.

▲ Rossius and Thys swiftly took the lead.

Vermandel pops hard to Dijon, but is barely three seconds ahead of Thys-Rossius that evening with Lenaers. The smaller the differences, the more the eyes of the Brusselsian shine. Vermandel is also the strongest towards Lyon, but Rossius skilfully sticks to his wheel. Thys posts himself in front of the inexperienced Lenaers. The overall win is in.

Philippe Thys beats Vermandel in the sprint of the 1921 Critérium des Ashes. ▶

With this fine win in his pocket, Flup is at the centre of the vedettes at the start of the Tour de Longchamps. This prestigious 100-kilometre trial saw the light of day back in 1885 and will live on as the Criterium des Ashes. The best like to lay themselves flat there in the autumn. The race itself is more important for snacking at the banquet afterwards, than for punctual cycling history. The preliminary programme includes roller skating and dog races. Parisian performers ride a gentlemen's trial. The party at Longchamps (also a hippodrome) is a lot like Waregem Koerse. Those who get to ride along or be there are among the lucky ones. Vermandel is already best off on the three-kilometre circuit without turns. Egg aims to follow. Then Pélissiers, Brocco and Thys come on. At the half-hour mark, they are already 24km away. Brocco has to go, while Aerts does a clever remount. The final sprint approaches. Thys is in the pincers of the left-wing brothers. The pace stalls. Philippe braces himself. Many

chances he will be flicked. Vermandel brings relief. He joins after break and sets up the sprint by surprise. Thys sees through the plan. He was waiting for it and creeps into the wake. On the line he can beat the devilishly strong René. 100 bornes and 2h 22. Philippe of old was not empty-handed at the end of 1921. In Doullers and Sanremo, he might still be thinking about the Tour, but with certainty he was already thinking about Lyon and Longchamps. Philippe of today once did the same when he was forced out of the wheels in a fledgling team time trial. Still looking forward to the Ardennes week, but knowing it had to happen in the Vuelta and on the Cauberg.

Thys, Buyze and Pélissier reopen Brussels' winter velodrome. Flup then heads south in a hurry. With no spring and Tour in his legs, he may continue in Milan-Modena and the Giro di Lombardia. On the Milan piste, Thys and newcomer Reboul - winner of

▼ Philippe Thys enjoys the overwhelming attention after his victory in Lonchamps....

Paris-Brussels that spring - are fastest. The race to the Balsamic resort is a warm-up for the autumn classic. Thys will once prove that he can also win elegantly, without strutting across the finish line. He does not reach the finish line in Milan and strunks much earlier than in 1917. The limestone boulders of the Alpi Bergamasche take out his legs. Masseur Panosetti has a week to get him fit again. Thys-Linart ride a three-hour pair ride at the Marseille track. The meeting flops across the board as the officials are not up to speed and spend the whole afternoon on a wine drip.

And then... Thys does something we are not used to from him. Another country omnium is scheduled in Nice. Van Bever has come over. The course is known concrete, until the organisers come up with a special interlude. There appears to be a short stayer trial on the bill: always fun for the public. No way: is Thys's first reaction. The old Georget challenges Philippe. Van Bever soothes the mood.

Cautious Thys wipes the sweat from his neck: a fully-fledged pro should be able to finish that and, all in all, it can't be any worse than riding down a col, can it? The control freak takes his chances. When things start to settle down, a swish follows. Georget and Azzine ride away from him for full three laps. In the second moto Philippe gives up and at the third attempt he rides stiff with the handbrake on. Six laps is the difference, over barely 10 kilometres. The Brussels bike show is over. Then the track can open again. The men of the tramway strike. There are 5,000 bikes against the long façade on Bertrand Avenue.

Together with Jef Van Bever, who lavishly circulates the stayer story, Thys continues his winter programme. Several more performances follow in Paris. After the New Year, far away from journalists and opinion makers, the urge arises to go for it all over again. They are not yet rid of the triple Tour winner...

◀▲ Philippe Thys during the 6-hour race in the Brussels WIntervélodrome.

▼ Philippe Thys during the "Prize F. Faber" at the Paris Pershing stadium. From left to right: Goethals, Bellenger, Alavoine, Barthélemy, Lambot, Scieur, Thys and in the second row Mottiat.

1922

Splashing up-
goose fat

Preparation for the 1922 round is classic cake; lots of practice and little racing with Baugé's approval. The death of his sister doesn't sit well with Flup. So young still. What is to become of little Philippe now? He cannot offer much support on the home front. Duty calls. In March at southern training camp, playfully complete the Mont Chauve and Angel climbing races and build up to Paris-Tours and wait for the first big test.

Thys followed the group arriving three minutes after the prize beasts. The skinny Pélissier has the early muguets firmly pressed into the palm of his hand. This is necessary as he pushed off in the sprint to brother François. Then again, to copain Brunier, who may become French champion in return. No one files a complaint. The daredevils are already getting away with it. Philippe creeps into the shadows. At Bordeaux-Paris they see him pass at kilometre 350, then he suddenly disappears from the radar.

The hilltop village of Francorchamps, gets gentlemen of rank and file who see bread in a wooded race track. Close to the famous spa town of Spa, the bolides are sure to attract interest. Motorbikes occupy the circuit in 1921. For car racing, it will be

◀ The 1922 Belgian Championship is held at Spa. Thys tries to escape but is caught by the strong teamwork of Scieur, Beeckman and Lambot. In the sprint, Vermandel puts Thys at a bike length. Sellier, Rossius and Scieur complete the top 5.

a year's wait. In the promotional budget for the Grand Prix, there is also the setting up of the Belgian Cycling Championships. Another week until the Tour. Now things get serious.

Thys secretly nudged the course. The course must suit him. It is a lap with only two tasks: descend and push. Despite the many altimeters, 12 storm to the finish line. This is mainly the work of Philippe, who eagerly chases everyone in the finale, making himself suspect. Mottiat hits the ground in full sprint and disrupts everything and everyone.

Vermandel wins and Thys is in the most despicable place. Coming second is nice in any race, never in a championship. Philippe had kept all the pressure off, declaring for weeks that he would only participate in the tittelren as a courtesy. It had been a lie. He had lain awake at Francorchamps, hatched a plan to take the jersey and let the colours do the talking at the Tour start.

The plan fails and reaching Le Havre behind is not a good start, although it is still not too bad versus the rivals. Nothing is lost. Just as well, because isn't it quietly the Tour of Last Chance? With stage win in Olonne, time is gained back. Philippe smiles. The sky clears. The French last won their Tour in 1911. That's an element to take into account. They are on a roll this year. Every national stage win is hugely gratifying. Bellenger wins from Thys in the sprint and Jacquinot already has his second stage win in Brest. The old Christophe has to put on the yellow once more and along the Atlantic coast Jean Alavoine is going like a hornet stung. At the foot of the mountains, he is closing in on leader Christophe and Thys.

At Peugeot they are not very talkative in 1922. The team counts Belgians employed by the Brussels man. Thys negotiated that way. Otherwise, few consignments are given. There is an unmistakable France et les autres atmosphere at the table every evening. Chauvinism is close at hand. From whom the French outcry should come is unclear. The team stocks only jumpers: Jacqui, Bellenger, Degy and Alavoine. French classification riders are thin on the ground, perhaps Gars Jean is the most eligible.

Cultured Jean is an impulsive sprinter at the start of his career. Later, he retrained himself as a bagarreur and classic rider. Climbing remains a tender spot with the elo-

▲ The peloton passes Maaseik in the Tour de Belgium.

▲ Winner Vermandel.

▲ The riders wriggled through a narrow lock crossing in Loosen.

quent prankster and he has never managed to persevere in the Tour. He has too small an engine, which always sputters and stalls in the second half of the lap.

Alavoine is a clean athlete and a causeur par excellence, who seems plucked from Parisian salons. Gars Jean always takes the floor on behalf of the peloton when it comes to regulations and decisions. The erudite formulations with which he makes his point never fail to move Desgrange. An amusing debate of words amidst the cultural Tour wasteland is to his liking. That le causeur, usually uphill, starts his story and then hangs lustily on the link of Le Cercueil (nickname for the director's car) leaves the otherwise callous race director cold.

Peugeot bosses are under public pressure. The French must win. One must not suppress the popular will this time. The Lion brand has to think exclusively domestic for a while. They don't really want to break their promise, but still ... Thys retains his free role, but must stay close to Christophe. In Bayonne, he is still just eight minutes behind Gaulois and well ahead of Alavoine. However much the charming showbiss star André Perchicot tries his best to make everyone smile during a big performance, the atmosphere remains tense. The Bayonne pistier crashes his plane in WWI and breaks all the good bones in his body. He retrains as a singer and releases the funny Sérenade de la Pureé.

Thys will spend his life hiding behind one unlucky day in the Pyrenees, the trip on which he ended up in Perchicots puree. Just when a fourth victory seemed to be falling into his lap, suddenly it all went wrong. Masson sr. passes on to son Emile the meticulous account of the legendary Bayonne-Luchon stage of the 1922 Tour. It is first-hand information, written out in Francs Massons, mon père et moi. The stage will crumple the pronostics papers and sideline Thys for another Tour victory. Could it be that he himself was instrumental in throwing away his chances of a fourth degree that day?

The day does not start very well. Desgrange jeers at the French. In his editorial, he lectures Jacquinot - who could not stomach the loss of his yellow jersey to Christophe. Jacqui needlessly attacked Cri-Cri and thus abandoned les intérêts de la patrie. The fear that Thys will benefit is not in so many words in his warning. But the Tour boss's discours de rassemblement is unfairly about the lidless Belgian. France, as usual, sees Thys sitting on a somewhat hidden yet close branch like a bird of prey looking around quietly.

A clear moon is shining over the land of Basque hats. That means as much as a cold night when riders are unsure how many layers to put on. It is that vestimental problem that will bring overheated Masson to Thys. When the sun squeaks, the woollen leggings come off. At that striptease, the Tour heroes cycling stick their shoes between their teeth. At the bottom of the Col d'Osquich, Thys already has to change a tyre. At the summit, he is back in the lead and even turns first up the Aubisque.

After the first pentes, he suddenly feels unwell. A shrinking stomach starts throwing up acid. Bah! Drinking water, walking upright, sitting down, airing burps ... It doesn't help. Alavoine did not wait and went on the attack for the third day in a row. He knows why. It is now or never and the Peugeot leadership will not whistle back at him. Thys gets back on the wheel of yellow Christophe and leaves him behind. Higher up he pays for that effort again and has to get off the bike.

Alavoine crossed the misty summit 12 minutes earlier, but nothing is lost yet. Whoever rides in yellow gets all the teammates to serve. As long as that is not the case, in principle everyone goes his chance. Thys must therefore put Christophe at a sufficient disadvantage and watch out that Alavoine doesn't get too far away. If that fails, he can shake it off for now in the current Jeanne d'Arc climate.

▲ In the 1922 Tour de France, Alavoine and Thys ride up the hill of Poix.

Philippe is leaking again on the descent of the Aubisque and has to go into the red on the flat to contain the damage. In Aix-les-Thermes, he gives up 20 minutes. What happens between the cols is little exposed. Yet those passages are the great mystery of the day. They will remain so, as telegraphy is down throughout the 65 (Department Number) that afternoon and journalists have been riding ahead to order un gigot percé au romarin sauvage in time. After all, they could only be in one place at a time and riders who despise in the mountains lie about it in the evening anyway. Thys seems to be stabilising, but has tyre failure yet again. In Lourdes, the difference is half an hour. A gush of holy water won't change that anymore. Alavoine is still flying forward. Philippe rides like a yo-yo. It rarely happens to him, but out of control he is not at his strongest. On the Aspin, his rear wheel breaks. Is all the carefully avoided Tour bad luck from a long career now foisted on him en vrac?

Masson and Thys arrive at the Biggore supply 45 minutes after the leader and half an hour after the elite group with Christophe. It is 1.40pm. They take their time to step into a restaurant. Masson to dine, slack Philippe mainly to recuperate. As they are about to leave, teammates Bellinger and Jacquinot arrive. Thys - still vomiting - and Masson decide to wait until the French have eaten.

Things are amiable, although Flup has to lie down on a bench regularly. Finally, the four of them leave the town at 3pm in the direction of Campan's forge. Procrastination is not Thys's style. Masson's diary tells of the French quitting a little later and from then on, he and Philippe have a fun afternoon. Like two bad boys, they trek through desolate mountain country. Flup at times cynically exuberant, nonchalant for his liking and not even attentive to the state of the road surface and the braying of the crowd.

On the Peyresourde, at the suggestion of a shepherd, they go to try out a shortcut to the summit. It is a wrong guess. The garrigue is buzzing with horseflies. With rolling stone chips under their feet, the adventurers full of scratches and swollen spider bites finally make it to the straight and narrow. They have lost more time than gained. In Luchon, the clock ticks full three hours after Alavoine's arrival. Then both freebooters arrive. The Brussels man sick and empty, promptly looking for a bed to plop down in, but not really turned on. Could Thys really not have done better, or did he flip a switch somewhere along the way and resign himself to the confluence of circumstances: a bad day for him and a flawless moment for his teammate competitor? It can happen to an athlete under pressure: snap, throw in the towel and let things

▲ Alavoine in front of Sellier and Thys on the ascent of the Izoard.

▲ The newspaper caption reads, "The track is not rideable regarding it."

PHILIPPE THYS EXAMINE UN CARRÉ DE CHOUX
DANS LE JARDIN QU'IL VA BIENTOT QUITTER

run their course. For those who can't make sense of the facts, the sloppily displayed Tour Market always has baskets of outlet anecdotes and chunky suppositions ready: to grab criss-cross from.

There is the story in which Thys, Lambot and Scieur - effectively a triumvirate with plans of their own when it came down to it - are the targets of sustained persterism that year. Thys poisoned and therefore so ill? In a later interview, Philippe says: that a bought-out Peugeot attendant flicked him at the summit of the Tourmalet. He has the frivolous trip with Masson noted in the same interview, but places the story in 1924. However, the Walloon was off course before the mountains that year.

Masson, for his part, also ferments in his book the possible poisoning of Thys, but sets the story in 1922. In that year, however, the caravan did not cross the Tourmalet in extremis because an avalanche had deposited debris. Poisoning was a regular occurrence, but therefore also immediately invoked by riders as a cause of indisposition. No one ever cried out loud that it was overtly sabotage, and Thys did suffer from sudden stomach problems more often during his career. The clinical picture during the mountain stage was very similar to previous meltdowns; near Chimay and on the Turbie. The story of the poisoned gift first surfaced after Perpignan, while other papers attributed the cause of the débâcle to eager drinking of ice water near Lourdes. But there is another fact that has been fiercely under-reported: a medical problem that had to remain hidden from the outside world in 1922. Philippe has toothache after Olonne and does not sleep a wink. Medication brings no improvement and the unkie molar has to come out. There are no specific dentists so far away from Paris. The operation has to be done at a GP's office. The tooth left behind at the foot of the cols is nowhere considered a possible culprit.

Philippe says he: still lying dead on his bed on the rest day, thinking of giving up, but suddenly feeling hungry in the evening and able to keep a meal down. The period is over. Couldn't the appetite have returned a little by the pleasant coolness of a fan of large banknotes? The Brussels man does not often make bold moves, but when he has to, he is a master at turning temporary incapacity into some advantage.

▲ In Metz, Philiipe gets new tires and the newspaper during the rest day.

NOUVELLE SÉRIE. N° 108.
Le Numéro : 50 Centimes.
ÉTRANGER : 65 Cent.
Jeudi 27 Juillet 19..

LE MIROIR

DES SPORTS

IIIII PUBLICATION HEBDOMADAIRE ILLUSTRÉE, 18, RUE D'ENGHIEN, PARIS IIIII

Photo de notre envoyé

LAMBOT MONTE LA CÔTE DES BOIS DE MOLLE AU COURS DE LA DERNIÈRE ÉTAPE DU TOUR DE FRAN..

..vainqueur du seizième Tour de France, soucieux de conserver sa première place du classement général, s'est sagement ten..
..rement en arrière du peloton de tête durant la quinzième étape Dunkerque-Paris, à la fin de laquelle il est arrivé quinziè..
..h. 38' 35''. Le temps du Belge Lambot pour les quinze étapes est de 222 h. 8' 6''. Alavoine, deuxième, a totalisé 222 h. 4..

1922

Ravages of time?

Thys can slog through mire and hardship just fine, but it remains a coquettish filou always and everywhere. Flup has definitely lost the Tour, he is that realistic. But surely there is no more leading role waiting, as there was for Buyze in 1913? He needs to act fast, with Alavoine still not wearing the yellow in Luchon. Besides promising not to get in the Frenchman's way, negotiations earn him a free role for stage wins. Agreements are agreements, but in the race everything is elastic and trucable. Gars Jean continues to act strongly. On the road to Perpignan, he pushes aside the old Christophe - who suffers from't sciatic.

Peugeot has finally got the yellow, but is everything and everyone behind the Frenchman now? Alavoine has been around long enough to doubt that. Right he is. Philippe already reminds the team management of the deal, winning in Toulon and again the day after in Nice. Are they symptoms of honour or is there revenge at play too? From the first signpost to the Greek bathing spot, everything always runs smoothly. Flup takes Alavoine for a rash raid through the spiky interior. It will earn the leader extra minutes. Is it a heartfelt nice gesture from the guide? There are also elements to build a different story with, insinuations that Thys rode the proud yellow jersey - which certainly did not want to undercut it - on his chosen terrain as wriggly as a soft sandwich. To show who was the best tour rider? The fanatical press kept cherishing the vicious account for a long time. The course of the ride does not support the thesis of the quatons.

In that ninth stage, to Nice, Alavoine is the first to attack on the Col de Braus. Lambot follows. Thys has to chase and only joins later. From then on he pushes hard for kilometres and puts Lambot in trouble. After a flat tyre on the descent to Sospel, the Walloon had to drop out for good. Alavoine and Thys remain and start the Castillon together as model teammates. On the piste of Pont-Magnan, Philippe is in a lost position, until a cale-pied comes loose on the Frenchman in the penultimate bend and the right pedal bounces off the concrete ringing. Thys is definitely no better that day, but wins by a stroke of luck. Which does not rule out, that Alavoine did too great too many days in a row and so slowly exhausted himself.

Lambot, Christophe, Lenaers and Beeckman were set back considerably in Nice in the classification. The race does not lock up in the Alps, which would have been the obvious thing to do. Philippe continues to chase Alavoine. His appetite for attack always sucks someone from the classification. The leader has to react attentively every time. Towards Brainçon, where Thys loses on the Allos with new stomach problems, his urge to be the first to round the new climb of the Vars and the Izoard outweighs the discomfort. Not even a nasty puncture can stop Flup. He drags Alavoine's direct attackers into a rock-hard adventure.

Bottecchia is the victim of a dirty trick. Someone shoves a witch's mixture into his hand and the good-for-nothing is oblivious. Soon he is vomiting his way through the Case Deserte, but the buffalo is not to be trifled with. Does Thys see in this the ultimate proof that, as a foreigner, he too must almost certainly have been a victim of poisoners? Evil and injustice haunts his mind and he curtsies even more fiercely. Gars Jean has no choice, he must follow. Powers are again flowing away that he will later come up short.

At the top of the fortified town of Briançon, Thys wins again. Alavoine stays on for a long time and, all in all, still looks fresh. His lead over Lambot is intact. But in a harsh stage from Briançon to Geneva, over the Galibier, the leader is lonely on foot. It is wintering on the roof of the Tour, with slush and biting winds. Alavoine had to change tyres. Then his chain jumps over the pions every so often and gets jammed each time. The 22-minute lead is largely lost. Thys can't help as he stands warming his icy hands in innocence on the radiator of a follow car. Lambot hides and - mindful of Jean's weaker second half of the Tour - begins to calculate his own chances once more. From Geneva, another day of misery begins for Thys. Unwell again, he has to regularly dismount and dive into the bushes on the way. The strength literally drains away. The top ten washes away with him. The impossibility of assisting the yellow jersey is made clear early in the stage. Sorry.

Alavoine suffers another puncture in the full finale and his lead is further cut short. The candle goes out completely in Alsace, where he will lose over an hour due to as many as six tyre changes. Thys, as well as Lambot - who is only a few minutes behind - are never around to rescue him. Have they rehearsed French inventiveness? They dredge up a clean explanation and invoke regrettably convincing excuses all the time.

▲ Lambot and Heusghem on the road.

The team has degenerated into a basket of crabs. Everyone understands they are out with a batch of bad tyres at Peugeot. What is the cause of that? It has never been seen at the secure superteam. Are there - as Thys pointed out but placed in a different setting and year - bought-out personnel in their own ranks? Alavoine, with 50 punctured tubes, is very badly off.

When the calf towards Strasbourg egg is so after drowned, Lambot is ordered to wait for leader Alavoine. This puts Hector Heusghem narrowly into yellow. He already smells the oil balls of Paris. Peugeot hits the ball wrong again: the yellow is gone. The robust Carolo has no more helpers at his disposal, though. His older brother is still in the race, but Louis drives for Peugeot. Baugé puts him under guardianship. The loser is not even allowed to ride near his brother.

Hector's scarf doesn't spin in the back wheel. Oficially, his own brutality does him in. He dives over a pathetic mangy dog, who is chased across the road by the desperate competition with a kick to his rear. After sampling his hobbled Thomann, Heusghem quickly takes a new bike. That's swearing in Desgrange's church. Race director Dupont demands the bike for inspection and puts it on the train towards Thionville.

Still the folly has not reached its peak. After arriving in Metz, - dixit L'Auto - a technician is caught in the presence of the leader further damaging the confiscated bike. In an attempt to secure a pardon? The Thomann entourage claims that the bike was misappropriated during the unguarded train transport and that neither Heusghem nor the team personnel were to blame.

The time penalty that awaits is huge and Lambot-Peugeot reluctantly take the yellow jersey the following morning. Life is for the daring. Thys keeps his mouth shut but thinks his way through. No one is bona fide and sincere in this round. Brothers Alphonse and Jean Thomann quarrelled before WWI and sold on their little factory to Gentil out of necessity. The latter let the brand exist, but never gave it any attention or budget. The trumpeting elephant on the logo is on clay feet and does not have the clout to hire off big ads in the boss's sports magazine. Peugeot can do that without flinching. Has the lion brand rectified all its accumulated blunders by buying the Tour? Never mind Philippe. The roads to Dunkirk look friendlier than ever.

When in Maubeuge it turns out that his fork is crooked there is no stress. It's not about winning this time. Isn't watching a rich portfolio the very best alternative to winning? Alavoine's impending loss is widely discussed in the French press. Frustration mounts and the foreign trio gets blame and surpluses thrown at their heads. The Ardennes cartel exists. Departing from Scieur, they often train together on the flanks of the Meuse Namuroise or the high peaks of Gedinne and already dare to cross the border at Givet, for a better glass of wine.

The friends keep up their climbing rhythm with what is available in the Ardennes. Baraque Michel is the country's point culminant at the time, as Botrange is still in the Empire. Lambot is initially furious with Thys: because the youngster is quick on the uptake and takes an immediate overall win in the 1913 Tour. Friendly sand is later sprinkled over that false start.

That the three did not needlessly counter each other's plans is obvious, but that does not mean they did not each ride for their shill (profit) when it mattered. The three Belgians were friends, but they had no redeemable bank account. With Frenchman Alavoine, however, they had even less in common.

Would rational Philippe have been viciously vomiting at the roadside? It tends towards the bad in man to deceive Gars Jean like that. Surely Thys was not like that. How it can then be explained that his physical preparedness was excellent one day and then lousy the next remains a medical mystery.

The disillusionment surrounding 1922 lasted a lifetime. Flup entrenched bitterness behind the confluence of nationalism, deceit, illness and bad luck. But if, despite all that, he had kept pedalling to Luchon instead of throwing in the towel, only an hour

Dimanche soir cette course individuelle de 100 km. a vu la victoire de René Vermandel (au milieu), en 2 h. 39 m. 21 s., suivi de Philippe Thys (à droite) et de Jean Brunier (à gauche).

Rossi VIN APÉRITIF — LES PRÉFÉRÉS DES SPORTSMEN — VERMOUTH Martini

▲ The top three of the 100 km track race pose for the photo. Jean Brunier, winner René Vermandel and Philippe Thys.

would have been lost that day. Maybe a little more. Given the follow-up in the Alps and the bad luck of many others, definitely not an unbridgeable gap.

Firmin Lambot navigates the smoothest through the intrigue and disaster and will once again be overall winner. He is the first in the Tour's history to become laureate without winning a single stage. It is the Tour de l' injustice and unfairness will never again surface. Eugène Christophe, after the early failure of Thys, finally looked set

▲ Brussels-Sportif members pose in front of the trophies they brought in during the 1921-1922 cycling season.

to win. As in 1913 and 1919, his fork breaks and he has to continue on a pastor's bike. The surprising Jean Alavoine then gets his hands on excellent papers. Too many punctures and too few friends will kill him too. Finally, Hector Heusghem has too little influence and too small a team.

Baugé's troops are back in line due to circumstances and towards Parc des Princes they will not let anyone solo. Rossius, Sellier, Masson, they are all ready to reap fame with a cat's leap. Yet Thys sticks his hefty mug forward and races across the finishing line first. Dotting the "i" of incontournable. He signs the final race sheet with dots on the "ij". Why Thys always hand-signed as Thijs, no one knows. Was the ypsilon an overly stylised whitewash of his Willebroek origins?

That same autumn, he still wants to prove that the intestinal system was liable for false ratios. The clutch Grand Prix Sporting is the course of choice to set an example. Philippe - staged by Peugeot, of course - will ride the course with ... Alavoine. Thus, the instigators of enmity are suddenly full of wind. The impossible occasional team takes victory in Lyon after sublime teamwork. Peugeot is suddenly no longer a national ministry, but a flexible international company that must make profits and universal progress, regardless of standards and borders.

Philippe did not want to give up and rode the best track winter of his career in Brussels. After a second place in the prestigious criterium of road racing, several victories in Americaines followed with Vermandel and the young Pierre Rielens, who was nicknamed Pikke Vlam (Fat Flame) because of his fantastic leg speed and jump.

1923

Theo time?

In the head of Thys no one has ever managed to look. However, it does seem that in 1923 he decides to embark on the next episode of his racing career. It is time to cash in on name and fame and let go of the urge to deliver top performances. He will focus on daily successes. A bicycle model bearing his name is in the pipeline and Philippe married the 12-year-old Marie-Thèrese Van Keerbergen between Christmas and New Year's Eve 1922. Although racing is a far cry from her bedtime show, she regularly accompanies Philippe to races.

They have been dating for a while. Not on the sly, but neither via the rolled-out carpet at the front door. Father is a stiff notary's clerk in Halle and not too keen on his daughter's lovemaking with a racing driver. But Thys's sweetheart is a self-confident madam. She pushes through her will saying: if it doesn't work out I won't be at your door again daddy, rest assured. The couple move from Transvaalstraat to a modest Art Deco house in the nicer Limbourglaan. A street full of trees and better citizens.

The white wedding light turns the gloomiest winter in the observations of the RMI. Young marrieds don't need weather forecasts. The first classics fall early and require a lot of winter preparation. There are domestic and business obstacles. For the first time, Thys does not live for sport alone. For the good of the soldier's pack in the occupied Ruhr, he does want to take part - for the good cause - in a few races with Vermandel. The chilly Tour of Belgium remains on the sidelines. Philippe heads to the sun-ripened Circuit du Languedoc. When he leaves home, the continuation of the family tree is a fact. Thys will become a proud dad in the autumn.

In Montpellier, he is too relaxed and victorious. Piquemal, a driven regional, does not allow himself to cross again. Bellenger takes the lead and in the final stage Flup limits himself to assisting his teammate. The preparation for the round contains only assignments for other Peugeots. It feels different. There is no more eagerness and inner nervousness. Thys needs to recharge to leave for the Tour start in Paris. That has never happened to him in a healthy condition.

Beyond a third place in the stage from Brest to Les Sables d'Olonne, the spirit does not reach further. The head is full of mice and the legs just dangle from it. They wallow on autopilot, with no guidance. In the mountains, it's muddling along on routine. In Toulon, where the ride to his favourite city Nice begins, the room door stays shut. There are constant rumours of wantonness en route, sabotage attempts and threats against the Belgians. Flup stands in opposition to his renommée, just hours away from the leader. There is no more honour to be gained here. Heusghem and Lenaers feel the same way and are grateful coupé companions on the way back to Brussels.

Last year, Philippe last had a serious stab at overall victory. That dream then broke down on the way to Luchon. Full of adrenaline, he then wanted to show who was the best and racked up four more stage wins after the Pyrenees. It will remain his last great tour de force; one that could be placed alongside that of the heroic Buyze in 1913. Right, gentlemen journalists?

Henri Pellisier revisits his decision never to meet Desgrange again. It does not take much for the two to cross swords again and again. When the Tour boss goes over the list of contenders for round wins in spring, he makes the bold statement that Pélissier can be dropped immediately because he cannot give up. That is enough to lure Henri out of his hole. He wins the 1923 Tour de France, driven as never before, with telling ease and wide lead over teammate Bottecchia. That a guilty hand poured arsénique into Scieur's drinking can as an interlude before that, and secretly worked Lambot's pedal with a hacksaw, is only a minor afterthought. France finally has a winner again, 12 years after Garrigou. That is the important thing. The monthly edition of L'Auto sold out before noon.

The build-up to 1923 Paris-Lyon has begun. Training work on the Brussels home front alternates with speed tests on the Buffalo cycling track. Flup is still in demand and, at half-time, still dares to jump on the train quickly for an omnium France-Belgique. The team can continue to use him wherever it wants: but if the little one were to get off earlier he will give up. The Peugeot bosses laugh heartily and agree. Paris-Lyon, the longest one-day race of the year, turns into a nasty stormy affair. Frantz wins, but his mate is less so. Alavoine and Thys sneak into third and sixth, taking the duo classification again. Once landed in Lyon, the Tour du Vaucluse may become a compulsory number. Flup is around anyway. He does his job, but can no longer recharge and gets off complexly on the way. Philippe wants to go home: now. Reassured by the normal course of pregnancy, he still competes in Luxembourg, on the cosy track of Hamme-Zogge and the piste of Moustier-sur-Sabre.

The Belgian inter-club championship in Brussels can still be added. Antwerp BC is far too strong. The Pajols finish in the belly of the standings. Back home the same evening is the motto. The famous team chrono is an annual autumn assignment out of club love. Thys has long been without a permanent home in Brussels for his marriage and at times spends more time in the Ardennes and Paris, than in the capital. Relocation does not matter, whenever Brussels Sportif asks, Philippe comes to the Cinquantennaire.

September 30's GP Wolber is a compulsory number. Will it still succeed? Thys starts dreaming. Flowers for wife and child? Imagine. You never know how the race will go? Riding along can open perspectives. Dreams are deceiving. Masson knocks off Pélissier. Thys is never able to follow the better ones after Compiègene and would have been better off riding home from the North.

On Tuesday 16 October, little Theo is born. It is a boy. The gender is then still a surprise that young parents have to wait for. With the slogan: as long as it is healthy, preference is waved away. In 1923, being born healthy gives considerably more prospect of a carefree life. Those who have a problem from the start often have to resign themselves to Darwin, seven lit candles and beewegen notwithstanding. For those who cannot join the fittest, little science and equipment is available.

Everything is fine with the sprout. He will grow up with Disney Studio - for which the brothers Walt and Roy put the first lines on paper that day - and not lack anything. Maman and Philippe can enjoy themselves for a while. They are a strong couple, gradually becoming an unbeatable twosome. She knows her stuff, can lead on the home front and manage staff. That will be an asset when they will run the bus company together and her men are frequently away from home.

Thys remains a bread rider for a while and is on the lookout for easier money-making opportunities. Along the way, he quietly ogles lucrative pursuits for after cycling. Philippe is not a flemish housefather and husband, but a precise and responsible family man. The family needs to be in order: clean clothes, fine shoes, tender meat, sugar and white bread will never be lacking.

In the Brussels Derby, he doesn't finish anything and in the Aces meeting, daddy gets rolled in the opening minutes. Thys takes up the chase. Noblesse oblige, but the fury is short. To mark l'Armisitice (armistice), Thys squad races with Vermandel in Paris. Train tickets are arranged. Cycling life resumes. Colleagues will jeer him. Surely Le vieux jeune père is going to treat sometime?

▲ Vermandel and Thys at the 1923 Paris-Brussels registration.

▲ The Tour de Belgium 1924. Masson, Thys and Verschueren sign the control sheet in Echternach.

1924

For whom the bells toll

· ·

The 1924 Tour de France must share attention. In the city of lights, the summer Olympics are in preparation in which Tarzan will swim to gold medals. Meanwhile, the world has to absorb shocking events: a putch in a German beer cellar, Lenin dying, Labour taking over the Empire and a first female minister, Nina. Frightened, the men look on. What are we all going to get next?

On the night of 21 June, the peloton sits side by side feasting in a resto on the porte Maillot. It is a bit cramped, but food and wine are excellent. Despite tighter time-frames, even more tourist riders have turned up than in other years. Geneva has been scrapped. The Francs Suisse is too expensive. At two o'clock they dash off: fauves storming out of the city, keeping the citizens of the banlieus and the first villages champêtre from sleeping. Once a year, men lean against sleepy facades and very old ladies sit at dark front doors admonishing noisy and careless children.

Pélissier, reviled and revered in the same breath, gets credit again after his win last year. Unfortunately, he had to pledge allegiance to Bottechia. Automoto had a choice to make: redeem the Italian's leading position or leave him to the competition. Henri seems to have changed. He is milder and more often satisfied with what is achieva-

◀ Bottechia and Masson walk across a pontoon during the fourth stage of the 1924 Tour de France. The tourist-routier Lœw knocks in fresh tart forces.

ble. Ottavio leaves no stone unturned and wins the first day in Le Havre. The Frenchman is already in the pincer there and has to keep his word. Thys is with the main force for a long time, but a regrettable puncture causes a three-minute loss. The stage winner gets three on top every day as a bonus. In Cherbourg, Bellenger, a regular in the opening stages, wins. On the way to Brest, it's an early start: 16 hours of cycling. Thys puts himself at the front and closely follows all the moves. The esbattements through Normandy and Brittany are always chaotic and cost strength. In Coutances, the Pélissiers get the hang of it. The elder is checked in the morning by a zealous commissioner for wearing different jerseys. The dictatorship is not liked and Desgrange does not want to talk to Henri about it before the start.

Together with teammate Ville - twice runner-up and already with aching knees - the brothers plonk themselves down in one of the inns belonging to the SNCF's heritage. At the Café de la Gare, Albert Londres, who follows the Tour for Le Petit Parisien, is a grateful prey. The reporter is a novelist and knows nothing about the race. He seeks out the edges of the spectacle for his column. The brothers take it up a notch and paint a picture of slaves who, against the absurd rules of power-hungry cycling directors, do not have an inch of story.

Infested by colonial injustice, the journalist thinks he can jot down rewarding material for a Germinal on cycling. The quitters conjure up jars and pills and testify smoothly and gladly about the harshness of the stile: freezing feet, voided fingers, fallen out toenails and other systematic physical inhumanities. Desgrange should have known: the lidded stubborn family always has to have the last word. The stick has once again been found and above all, a servant's existence in the shadow of Bottechia skilfully averted. There is worse going on in La Douce than the acrimony of wealthy Pélissiers. Bakers' guests, out of a tray of 56 loaves, cannot even reserve one for themselves. They are so grossly exploited and underpaid that only strikes will help. Londres has stepped into the wrong place for an epic about forced labour.

Beeckman is euphoric after winning on the giant Brest track and hoists himself into a tie with Bottecchia in the standings. Thys gets ringed at the meet and files an immediate complaint. The bell did not ring at the start of the final lap. There are no set rules on arrival at a velodrome. Riders have to read the roadbook closely every day. Depending on whether the track is big or small, of concrete or cinder, different rules often apply and rain often changes the arrangements several times along the way. Philippe simply miscalculated. His fast legs are a bit off, but the rules are on his side. Thys is declared ex-equo stage winner. The following day, when Bot puts on a new tyre near Quimper, Thys and Frantz shake the tree at the behest of Peugeot. In Nantes, there is a carnival. The riders have to get off their bikes. The peloton cackles over an emergency bridge as the Loire breathes rhythmically in and out.

Alavoine accelerates when the Italian with the exploded wild man haircut can finally connect. Without success. The assembled Peugeot troops did everything they could to get rid of the yellow jersey wearer. In vain. Heading towards Olonne, calm returns and a calculated peloton turns the Tour management into another group sprint. Much to the boss's annoyance. Blue Sardine fishermen stand in shoals along the side and duck for flying tennis balls. France is competing well at Wimbledon, but not in her own Tour. The bakers end their mutiny and everyone can once again soak hard crusted breads in coffee to their heart's content: the only cure for tooth fracture. Baguettes did not originate with France. Only Paris and fashionable coastal and spa towns offer baguettes. This frivolité exclusive is a scarce product, copied from the Wieners and available only in pâtisseries.

Luxury is spontaneously dispelled during the 482 tedious kilometres to Bayonne. A night on and some more trying to sleep on the bike. There is little enthusiasm along the way. The cycling leaders haven't understood that the course is changing and the pioneer time is coming to an end. Philippe is poor and loses ground again in the nervous finale. The Gironde press cliches front-page teers thrown on high cols. Bottechia cannot wait and goes on the attack even before the green forests of the Tourmalet emerge. Complacently, he disposes of teammate Buysse.

In Barèges, his attackers follow at a far distance. Teammate Lucien passes after 15 minutes, Mottiat with Frantz and the strong Beeckman after the half-hour mark. Brunero further ahead and Thys a full hour later. Scieur and Defraeye gave up. It was in this setting that the Brusseler would have received his poison ivy. The story may not be true and, in any case, Philippe forgot to add that he had long since ceased to be a candidate winner in Bayonne in the morning. Ruling out that riders drank from a faulty bottle is impossible, even if there are official ravishment points and team personnel on the road. Even then, the athletes had fixed favourites and habits that the team catered to. Thys reached Luchon a good hour after the winner. A result perfectly in line with his results in the first half of the 1924 Tour. Thys rides the Tour because his contract and annual salary at Peugeot so provides. At best, he still hopes for a strong day or a sudden flash. The old medicine men are getting tired.

But when the thunderstorm erupts and the dogs can't be moved by sticks, their magical power returns. On his way to Perpignan, Bottecchia decides to finish his work. Alancourt dares to follow. Thys roots his way forward in the rain. For hours he scans the horizon. After a quick climb of the Puymorens, the roads dry up and he joins the leaders. Bottechia is greying mass with a big nose cone. The Italian overestimated himself and drinks cold stuff until his stomach muscle escapes. He rolls off the mountain in the zinc of the citadelle Mont Louis and begs from there to drift along at the back.

But Bottecchia is originally a poor farm boy who never gives away a piece of bread lightly. In the sprint, he shoots suddenly from under the darkness of the plane trees and whizzes to the finish line like an arrow. Victorious Philippe arrives too late. Word break. Thys was about to say goodbye to the course that made him a famous and moneyed citizen. He's been at it all day and now this. Philippe searches for a yellow jersey in the jumble of the finish. The coward has fled. Thys grabs his bike and goes in pursuit. In a little school serving as a dressing room, he finally finds the Italian and slaps an accidental empty bottle until the shards jump around. Thys is shocked. Aggression he has always managed to control well and often benefited from it. Bystanders intervene to prevent worse and drag him out of the classroom. Flup willingly allows himself to be removed and reassures everyone. The frenzy is over. Bottecchia - totally out of his milk - has crawled into a corner under a lectern.

It took until the late summer of his career before they got Thys really angry. Soon it's off to Nice. Then the game is on the line. On the short stage to Toulon, Philippe will rest and then sleep for a long time. He will go into a trance. Bacteria mania sets in. Le Petit Parisien's follow car has been converted into a driving lab measuring 19 million bugs per mètre cube of air. In that atmosphere, the resentful fighter will soon have to try to live up to it. Nothing is yet known of good and bad bacteria.
What worries Bottechia more than dust and all critters are the Italian tifosi who cross the border at Ventimiglia to cheer him on. Once outraged, his compatriots can do much to flout and cause even more havoc. Destruction of one's own figurehead is among the possibilities. Bringing down or forcing the Italian in the middle of the madness to a halt is a scenario best considered.

Desgrange allows leader to leave in a different jersey and escape happening political violence. That actua quote allows the Tour management to invoke heir power and only slightly violates its own regulations. The roadside will look for a yellow jersey and find none that day. Until the first crossing in Nice, things remain quiet. Thys knows the loop over Sospel like the back of his hand. With a tough Alpine task in the pipeline, it is hoped for windlessness among the classification riders. Philippe samples the group and makes a first push. Alavoine and Bot himself join in. He looks deep into the coward's eyes. Angry looks speak: are you going to struggle again? The flight falters. With this company, the old fart does not dare to push on. Then Alavoine is allowed to ride away, and nothing is put in the way of the two Italians who follow. Is the leader in the combine again after all? On the Castillon, Thys does a great remount and gets to the front.

It will have to be done with a knack: forcing feed every time it goes uphill is a great recipe. Alavoine and Brunero give way. Aymo is still in his shadow after the winding descent to the coast. Alavoine is normally no match in the sprint. Flup takes his precautions anyway, forcing the Italian on the Turbie, to pull out all the stops. It's all on for the spaghetti breaker.

Philippe Thys, he and no one else, walks into Nice with lengths of lead. Speaker Arnaud announces him from afar. To speak of a received victory is perhaps an exaggeration, although Frantz and Bottechia remarkably freewheel the finale. Whoever wants to win the Tour has understood that taking an angry Thys to the Alps is not a good scenario.

▲ Bellenger, Thys and Degy refresh themselves at the source of the castle of Grange dés Prés, near Pézenas.

Now that the old one has got his act together, he will fail to stir things up any more. Philippe performs mandatory numbers for the last time during the rest day: farewell visit to the bike depot and closing reception at the city council. Rather no fête aux crustacés. Team leaders implore and beseech their riders to look away from inviting platters of seafood. Fish, shellfish and molluscs de l'epoque enjoy a dubious reputation. They are fermenting bombs, often left for long periods in water that has been too brightly warmed and still end up on a plate. The Belgian team will once leave the Tour because big grilled anchovies had been on land for a while.

In the Alps, Frantz still tries to destabilise Bottechia. This succeeds only slightly. While Thys touches on the trip to Strasbourg in his catalogue. It's a gamble. There are always privateers on the coast on Julliet 14 and the Luxembourgers smell the terroir of the Moselle. Frantz finishes nicely that day and in the Paris park the Italian yellow jersey is eager and far too strong. Thys ends his - at least he thought so at the time - last Tour a good three hours after the winner.

His last stage win is enough for now. The glittering entry along the shores of his beloved blue sea are on his retina. When half Niçois are once again allowed to proudly display the magnificent silver - designed especially for the stage arrival each time - above the city: it works like an addiction. Riders sometimes bathe in inexplicable self-confidence or, on the contrary, get childlike phobias on certain sections. They are always there either good or bad. Thys always found the strength to take a little extra time off on the Azure Coast and thus tumbled into his role as an avid collector of the coupe. Before leaving for home, he takes another look in his suitcase, because in Paris you have to watch your back. The artwork is still in there ...

1924

Salad Niçoise

Nice is full of invisible sprinklers vaporising dazzling brightness and perfumed bliss. There is something joyeux about the interplay of sunshine and overblown herbal scent. In the Savoyard resort, Thys has often anchored his favourable starting position in reinforced concrete. He won no fewer than three Tour stages there and on his very first visit in 1911, the unknown Belgian came out on top of the Peugeot-Wolber Circuit.

Phillipe has little merit in his surprising leadership that day. Opponent Figuet grossly misfires in the sprint. The temperamental little guy with Professor Sunflower look, drives a level-headed Swiss into the fences just to win anyway. A silly move. The victory tastes sweet for a moment: a few minutes later like a sticky acid ball. Sent to the last place of the leading group, the southerner feels cheated to his little toe. Crying, dejected and then haughty again, he creates turmoil and theatre during the rest day. When the vans load up and transfer the riders' cardboard valises, Figuet's belongings are still lying on his bed dismissively untidy.

The race management doesn't budge and the failed baller decided to show up at café Pomol by three in the morning anyway. He must be near Valence anyway. Figuet, at 28, is especially stronger than Thys. He was demolishing and staggering Philippe. But lack of reason and patience, unexpectedly put le Belge in pole position. The roles turn. No one knows where youthful Thys' strength lies. Once positioned at the top, he hardens like steel and is still hard to push off his pedestal. Later, during his professional lap work, this will become apparent on several occasions. It earns him the nickname the Basset: by no means a reference to the long-eared dog breed that looks up low, bending over, orphaned and sad. It is not the British genetic misfit with knobby joints that is at the origin of the comparison, but the Fauve de Bretagne.

The French variant is a small nippy animal, likewise with sagging seat posture, but with a very inscrutable vive gaze. Stocky and compactly anchored on the saddle, Thys is certainly not the most stylish of the lot. Despite his low-slung position, he has a clear view over the opposition. A low centre of gravity that is always on his qui-vive, you don't tip over easily. His eye insertion is an additional weapon. Philippe looks blurry ahead in all his photos; far beyond the lens.

It is only a false dreamer, because no one manages to erase anything from the corner of his eye. Thys's pupils never betray intentions or feelings. The broad double chin is always smiling, a tad deceptively. Philippe is a driving enigma: a deep ocean. When the Brusselsian gets off the bike, his being suddenly takes on a more affable, humane colour. When winning, he already dares to reveal charm, fresh from the liver.

Every time Nice approaches, Flup's legs itch. Desgrange's circular course is founded on fixed values and notions. In 1913, he reverses the direction of travel and prints the road book for the next 25 editions. Only when an alcoholic cantoneer somewhere has neglected a trançon de route to such an extent that a horse can break its legs there, his collaborators consider a slightly different route. Adhering to an identical route works easily and is cost-effective. But on the Azuren coast, they are initially unsure what to choose: Aix, Marseille and Toulon all come to mind. Only the requirement that the sea must be true turquoise-blue is on record. Arriving in Nice, the Tour does something very unusual: a frivolous loop. To go crazy for once?

The course takes it through the hinterland: up to Sospel, over the Esterel, the Col de Braus and the Castillon. Via the Turbie, with views of Menton and Monte Carlo, one descends again to the palm promenade. The lap atmosphere in Nice is unique. It is always a bit like coming home. Expensive white dresses and pantaloons come to admire the riders, in numbers as large as the hot water distillers from the hotel cellars, olive pickers and newspaper boys. The build-up to the stage bears crunchy fruit at picking height of Thys. A calm run-up with no danger and climbs that many riders don't know what to do with. Tricky pimples, not long enough for real climbers and too tough for fast guys.

It is perfect terrain for organising exploits and feats of strength and shooting forward in one go. Those who go crazy should settle down quickly, because on the stretch up to Sospel there are three playgrounds one after the other. How often did Flup experience reporters' cars barrelling up to his wheel and nervous journalists noting Thys laché et en danger. He knew better. The ride challenges one to waste strength without much gain. In between the slopes there are long flat stretches, in which the mistral always wins over a loner. Yet every time there are gullible people who think they can make history, but get caught up in their ideal. In the ride through the dry Provence air, Monsieur Prudance is always at the front. It's a ride written to the tune of leep people: wait, dose and finish. Philippe likes to win a lot in Nice. He does it once as leader in the classification and later Tour winner: in 1920. Often, staying close to direct opponents and looking them straight in the eye at the finish is enough. That one look makes for a big bang. This is how Thys won the Tour psychologically on several occasions.

Stage victories involve many duties, especially in Nice. There are always long ceremonies and a full programme awaits during the rest day. From at the local Peugeot dealer to the drinking of Le Petit Niçois and then still to the exhausting staircase of the town hall. Philippe could put it into perspective: for the rest it was pernicious, but I was still the centre of attention, glass of champagne in hand - which I never turned down - and surrounded by shiny cups. There were guys who added another meeting on the velodrome on the rest day in Nice. Wynsdau and Hudsyn, fashionable people from Brussels who rode along as unkempt, went there to earn a franc. That way those guys kept something on the side. Winning was not the worst thing that could happen to you.

Only in his first participation did Thys blunder on the way to his ville preferée, when the Tour is still coming straight out of the Alps. At 35th in the stage result, his excellent classification goes to the dogs. The belief to finish even then close in Paris is ebbing away. A pity, because Philippe will still sneak closer in later stages and not even be far from the podium. Two more victories in his second hometown come later, when he has become an outsider and stage contender. In 1922, he squeezed all the frustration out of his body in the back hills. To this day, no one knows what caused this: the sick day in the mountains or the double game of the Peugeot entourage? Alavoine, yellow jersey and teammate is with him that day. Will Thys want to help him to the final victory there for good or cycle into total ruin? It remains an open question. Lemond and Hinault also had no problem with the pecking order at the press table until they were let go.

In 1925, his last Tour, the will is there to make it to Nice again, but his knee decides otherwise. The city will always remain his favourite medicine against la fatique du Nord. Thys goes there often and gladly and needs no city plan. The club Gambetta, Avenue Felix Faure, Le Riviera Glacier: it is known territory. Monsieur Millet from Peugeot, pharmacist Santoni, commissaire-en-chef Menard, they call out in chorus from afar. A less pleasant memory of Nice follows, later. Whoever asked Flup which moment evoked the cleanest feeling about the city got the surprising answer: the moment the jury fired off the piste test behind motorbikes.

1924

Zen

. . . .

Thys puts it all together after the closing metres of the 1924 Tour. He himself was ugly at the time; mocking others and brutally kicking hefty riders backwards as much as a quarter-day. But it comes hard, losing hours and not being able to do better. Having to focus on scarce good days. In Thys's time, only the podium counts. The newspapers don't dirty more lead letters in subsequent years' Tour rankings. He now falls outside the top ten. Even if immortalising the lowest decimal is a preservation process of later times, the awareness of quiet decline does something to a person. Many of his opponents of the time are worse off athletically by now, but still ... Defraeye was on his own at the start, unbranded and forgotten. Mighty Marcel even fled to America and had to eat out of the hands of the mafia bosses of the ovals.

With places three and five, both Lucien Buysse and Fil Beeckman are making considerable strides as Tour riders. Thinking that from now on the Tour is a job for the young, Philippe pulls the door of the Parc cloakroom shut behind him with relief. Rest is not yet an issue. As a record man, Thys is still at the top of the wish lists to participate in the post-Tour races. The Parc des Princes should once again serve as the setting. Le Petit Tour de France will cover 60 kilometres and the riders will simulate two refreshments on the lawn: to make it look almost real. For the public, it is real. Film footage of the lap usually does not circulate until winter. Flup fits for Paris-Lyon. The prestigious GP Wolber remains compulsory cake. With a monster sum of 15,000 francs for the winner, the late race has huge appeal. All countries bring their best riders to the start. The Wolber race will set the stage for a real World Cup at the end of the cycling year. Thys stands smiling happily at the Porte de Patin.

The incorrigible brothers fry it brown again. Great commotion, when the Pélissiers are undetectable mere minutes before the control closes. Forfait? They don't push it that far: n'est-ce pas Monsieur Thys? Philippe chuckles: they dare anything, those sakkerse Pélissiers and especially when the establishment is in the hands of L'Auto. Where they end up, nobody knows, but suddenly they are there anyway: chronologically late. They find this particularly funny themselves. Françis puts on a big mouth: is Monsieur Desgrange going to refuse us the start perhaps?

There is suspense until the finish, where Girardengo beats the great Pélissier. Defeated at home, Desgrange promptly writes that down as: the defeat of pride. Thys continues to make regular appearances in Paris in November and December. The Velo d' Hiver is the setting for a France-Belgium match on St Nicholas Day. The bank account thickens. In January 1925, Phillipe rides the six of Brussels once more. Purely by chance, because Klaas Van Nek crashes so hard in Berlin that he has to cancel.

Negotiations in the Bertrand Avenue offices set the stage. Flup gladly intervenes: mais soyons raisonnable ... not for free and not to come and quickly organise my own downfall. In the person of Dewolf, he drags out a fine teammate. The new track director -Van Hammée has given his sports palace in concession for the time being - knows Thys knows Thys. He has long understood the old one's appetite for it.

If Philippe comes to argue over a decent teammate, it is to make something of it. Both can be found on the front line all week. That Aerts-Van Kempen eventually settle the matter in their favour cannot be called a losing point. The generation that grew up on the road still with a 24-hour saddle seat has an advantage over younger explosive rider types in the 144-hour trials.

That will soon change. The directors will flip their programming and come up with shorter and faster songs. The revamped spectacle catches on and business - until the advent of television - runs on rade wheels. At every meeting, all the entrance guichettes open and shoeboxes full of money are carried to the directors' offices.

After archangel Gabriel becomes French pure speed champion at 40, Thys too will consider moving on. Gabriel Poulain flees to Berlin to avoid having to do army service. Country treason costs him his cycling licence. Then he just becomes a broadside pilot and drills his nose into the ground twice. The archangel does not die, quite the contrary. In 1921, Gabriel soars three metres off the ground with his velo-aviette. The hybrid of bicycle and aeroplane still suits him best. Aviette competitions proliferated across France for a decade.

Via a screw on the bike's rear sprocket, fantasists really try to break free from the ground and float for a bit. They would like to take off the 10,000 gold francs Peugeot is doling out. Poulain warily pockets them. It is not that suitcase of coins that Peugeot is short of to stay out of the red. The big brand has bet on automobiles, done a lot of research and built a new factory in Sochaux. Sales are not following suit.

The cycling team has become a collection of old grunts: still hugely popular, but no longer able to bring the course into the fold. It is a prime time to call it quits and abandon the expensive affair. When the Peugeot family is in dire straits, it always either comes to a business divorce or reunification. The bike construction is separated from the car group and the cycling team disappears from the scene.

Will Thys continue even in those circumstances or not? He has never raced for another house. Isn't it too late now to look for another team? Klavervier Automoto from Saint Etienne is still interested. Sports director Baugé -who has just released his training book Le Secret Choppy - insists. Flup can work there as an expert by experience. Without pressure. Philippe has to get Bottecchia, the Buysse brothers and the enfants terribles Pélissier - who are now three - through the same door. A fine proposition, were it not for the fact that it comes with a concrete demand. Thys must take part in the Tour de France one more time. The new employer wants to grab publicity and fill annonces with the three-time winner in the run-up to the big event.

1925

Luchon

·······································

Philippe has no intention of giving in. The Tour door is closed and just as well. But the idea of a tenth participation and a grandiose anniversary is heralded as a farewell party in the Versailles ballroom. Thys is massaged like a Wagyurund. He gets to say goodbye to the Tour everywhere and show off as an Automoto ambassador throughout France. All right then, on pure routine it will still work, at least if I get to wear the number 14 again: sounds the revoked decision. The assent already lacks conviction there. 14 is his back rag preferé. Flup will wear the number eight times and ride all his victory laps in the Parc with it.

The ultimate preparation goes wrong as early as April. During the Six Days of Paris, Frederickx swerves too wide in the corner. Philippe is in the wrong place and breaks his collarbone once more. Thys's career as an enthusiast is a story of many misfortunes. Tyre and bone fractures he also suffers as a professional at the worst moments of his career. Only in the Tour does he finally have luck on his side more than once. No need to worry. Thys knows how to prepare for the big tour. He never needed many race days to get into the rhythm. That gift remains, even in a veteran. Cycling will next take almost 100 years to believe and invest in training science hors course. There are 18 shorter stages on the programme. Les Sables-Bayonne will be cut. This creates Bordeaux as the arrival point. To the east, Desgrange still fails to make the tedious final week more attractive. The Alps are far from Paris and the organisers neither want to drop Alsace nor let go of Dunkirk as the penultimate stage venue.

◀ Mottiat keeps his spirits up during the second stage to Strasbourg, in the 1925 Tour de France.

Bottechia is again supreme in the opening stage to Le Havre. Alavoine, Thys and Bellenger run in together, at more than 20 minutes. Friends-time-mates Christophe and Heuseghem arrive even later. The journey along the beaches to Cherbourg is not carefree either. Philippe has to fix a tyre at the kick-off of the race final. The grinta is gone. It is no different the next day, when Bottechia calls for help and has to leave the leader's jersey to Benoit. Henri Pélissier gets off at Le Faou, aptly pronounced le fou. He exchanges his rider's uniform for that of mechanic, combs his hair back and drives on in a van.

On Breizhe roads, he definitely leaves the course he has struggled with more often than loved. During the Châteaulin climb, Thys already has to release the role. Does it all still make sense? All his friends from back then have grown too old with him for Tourtumult. He still enjoys it though: the crowds along the roads and the honking followers. His name echoes through the crowd as of old. Women in lace costumes and men in heavy velvet brave grey skies and drizzly chill. The mercury does not touch above 15 degrees for days. Evoking home scenes, Thys bites through the doubt: how would it be with Theo? Should I buy him a nice mini-train from JEP? Maman will be angling for a box of nougat in her next letter. So I must make it south.

Benoit saves his jersey by eight seconds. Thys, for his part, strolls to Vannes and makes it to the control in 82nd place, saved from a blameworthiness at the last minute. Now is that luck or bad luck? It seems too much for the Tour. The leisurely pace through the Pays de Loire to Olonne is a windfall. The seaside town welcomes the riders only out of politeness and because Desgrange likes to book the same table in a little restaurant there, according to annual custom.

New Luxembourger Frantz won for the second day in a row. Philippe recovered and sprinted to a fine seventh place. A second casino is in the pipeline. The city has other plans and will finally wave goodbye to the caravan. To the new intermediate port, the young Pélissier and Thys manage to pilot their Italian leader through Cubzac in ideal position. The finishing line is on the cultivated foothills of Bordeaux, where the vintners are gradually running out of land.

The Tour may not enter the city yet. The love spark has not yet overflowed. Automoto cracks a bottle of Côtes-de-Blaye anyway, to the happy ending. Old faithful Barthélémy - who lost an eye on the Tour roads - fails to show up at the Pont de la Maye. Philippe again loses a trusted companion de route.

In the steepness of the Moulin, Bottechia has no opposition. Thys is the last pawn to launch the leader uphill. Bot times Benoit out of yellow. The Tour rests and cues through the botanique: where hydrangeas grow thicker than cauliflowers. The judges of the Pyrenees rumble in the background. In Saint-Jean-Pied-de-Port, the sun rises for everyone. The Basque inns and terraces invite Thys, now much more than before. The race moves on. Philippe decides to follow. Adelin Benoit is afraid of no one and overconfidently chooses to attack. Bot has to join in and is gritted to death on the final climb. Benoit is again in line for yellow. Thys can live with a place in the belly of the peloton. He has ridden right past the security walls, looked into the abyss and enjoyed the scenery. It may be his last bike ride through the mountains. Below him, creamy herds and long-haired crabas - which provide fresh milk to the shepherds - frolic along with the charges. In 22, he had also looked down one floor and been

▲ Thys falls flat just before the finale of the first ride breaks loose.

▲ The "veterans of the Tour" at the head of the pack. Jules Deloffre, Jean Alavoine, Eugène Christophe, Philippe Thys.

able to soak up a little atmosphere: relaxing in the loss. Then, however, every so often a flurry of wrath and shivering restlessness crossed his mind, unable to find a valve.

Sun and hail alternate, while cycling fans are driven up the slope in buses to cheer on the lap spectacle. Is that where the Brussels native got the idea to buy a motor coach? Time for philosophising abounds. At the side of Jacquinot and the ever-smiling Mottiat, he paddles among the touristes-routiers to the valley. Dolle Benoit is already washed up. Who is this Walloon anyway? A fierce fellow, raised over the coal of the Pays Noir. Winner of Brussels-Liège and champion of Belgium as an independent. Someone who always wants to race. Strengthened the exit to his first Tour, with a second place in Paris-Brussels. Before the start to Perpignan, Thys greets Bellanger, Christophe and Alavoine. As Frenchmen, they have honour to uphold in their round and still give their all every day with a great warrior's heart, although it is quietly beating too fast to be in the spotlight. Still, Phillipe is secretly jealous. He is not a Frenchman and no longer finds the drive. Since yesterday, a fin de siècle feeling has taken hold of him. In the rain, he laconically puts his signature on the race sheet.

Someone there has already spotted that it is a casual goodbye scrawl. Passing the last house in Luchon, le grand Françis, looks for Thys. They confer, set foot and make a right turn. Jacquinot, standing alone at Dilecta, drives after them. Exit. Bottechia needs no help, recaptures the yellow that night and will smoothly make it to Paris. The hotel is informed, the suitcase bound for Brussels already neatly made. Darling Nice was still a goal, but emerging fluid in the knee makes reason prevail. Making it to the end of the stages might not have been a problem, but anyone who has ever flown double through the villages of the south is reluctant to relinquish status.

Philippe remains a born auto-protectionist. Enough is enough. Before things take hold, the man in question needs to use his wits. For the bank holidays, Brussels has put together a 12-hour course on the winter velodrome. The event lacks allure and a

▲ Franz fell. The signal for the Buyze brothers to start dragging at the head of the pack.

▲ In the Crau plain, the Tour de France riders pass a group of riders participating in the local "Circuit du Midi.

signboard to fill enough seats. The knee is rested and Thys is being paid handsomely to get into the saddle.

When Budts and Desmedt hook up, Flup dives over. After half an hour of recovering on a neutralised brit, he gets back on the bike. It doesn't work out. It goes black before his eyes and the pain is unbearable. Philippe has a strong suspicion of what is going on. Moments later, speaker Joseph - the Tenor of the Sports Palace - calls off that Thys has left for the hospital with une fracture de la clavicule.

PHILIPPE THYS

1926

Vauxhall parts

The steady demilitarisation of the Rhine province is giving the heart of the German economy a little oxygen just in time. The export ban has been nothing but shameful protectionist politics, packaged as punishment. Opel is the domestic market leader in motor vehicles and bicycles. In Russelheim, they have not waited to plan and modernise. The tyre mechanisation is on point. Mass production can start and will be at the throats of other European countries in both the car and bicycle sectors.

The French bicycle houses, complacently at the top for decades, face close competition for the first time. The German giant has invested heavily in innovative concepts and is launching civilian bike types that are lighter and more solid than all the others. To bolster its excellence in sales, they invest in a real cycling team at the AG, with German amateurs and Italian pro Gay as mentors. Grassin wins the world stayer championship on a yellow Opel: the discipline par excellence in which a bike has to show how reliable it is.

In 1926, Van Hevel, Vermandel, Bellenger and Belloni joined the racing stable. René Vermandel quickly rose to the top. He often goes on practice runs with Thys. Somewhere along the way, the question of whether Flup wouldn't sometimes like to go with him to the totally unknown Germany falls pardonably between his spokes. What should he do, two collarbone fractures later? With Theo growing like cabbage, it might be the ideal time to go into business, while his name still rings like a bell. Philippe still likes to cycle, but isn't that out of habit? In his mind, hasn't he secretly stopped being a full-time rider without admitting it? Every rider has appointment with that terrible moment. Holding on to the unpleasant realisation that it would actually be better to quit and bite the bullet ... and finally never quite be ready. Even Thys, who always knows so well what he wants, has a hard time of it.

With lucrative offers, Flup still sometimes wants to get his bike out. The family can live off it and the condition is still maintained daily. Enough to not be driven away anywhere, because the proud disposition would never allow that.

Negation and habit prevail. Philippe will not sign a one-year contract with Opel, but is willing to accompany Vermandel in a number of races abroad. On the home front, he will come out on the track between races. It is a compromise, a wind-down scenario with enough room to postpone the irrevocable for a while. Vermandel won't leave him alone. Whether Flup wouldn't mind depanelling them in Milan-Sanremo? Vauxhall has to fight on two fronts, what the same weekend there is also Tour de Vlaanderen. Freedom turns out to be relative. Surely we won't start that way: suggests Thys.

But the request also strokes his vanity. On 23 March, he stands monte in Milan and follows like a young colt well past Savonna. When at Alassio the pace picks up and things start to undulate too often, he lets the gang run on. Now Belloni has to pull his strand in the final. Mission accomplished. In the Stuttgart Kriterium, he will ride for Vermandel. Kriterium turns out to be the German translation of a course of up to 300 kilometres. Thys will ride in the main force to the line and has to scrape his friend René off the stones after a death-defying sprint. He certainly does not do the French classics. The Rundfahrt of Chemnitz at the end of June he does. Belloni takes the flowers and Philippe still wriggles his way into fifth place. Now the belt goes off for a while. Pistemeetings in Mariaburg, Genappe, Kortrijk and Sas van Gent keep the frame strong. If necessary, they practise every day on tours up to 100. Via Halle to the hills of the Borinage or together with Vermandel along the canal and Scheldt to Hoboken. When the lap for independents stops there, both are welcome guests who get attention, not the hobbled peloton.

Brussel Sportif can still count on Thys for the inter-club trial. Baudot has done a lot for him and that will never be forgotten. As the leaves fall and darkness sets in, the question of how to proceed once again arises. In 1927, Opel releases the brakes. With the ZR3, a racing bike in seamless steel enters the market unparalleled. The name refers to the popular Zeppelin of its own making, which smoothly crossed the ocean and gave New Yorkers a stiff neck.

The top manager of the cycling scene, Alphonse Baugé, is recruited. He gets to contract a selection of professional cyclists to say U to. The Frenchman searches his ad-

▲ Presentation of the Opel cycling team at the Rütt Arena. From left to right: Van Hevel, Gerard Debaets, Gaston Debaets, Jaquinot, Vermandel, Blanchonnet, Ville, Ibron, Sellier, Zanag, Belloni and Thys

dress book for the o-p-q-r-s-t ... sends a letter and asks for an interview. And whether in Germany they want the dreifache Tour-Sieger dabei wollen ... Philippe can't earn more anywhere at the end of his career than with the German giant-to-be. When Baugé arrives in Brussels and starts an exposé in his well-known style, Thys gives in. However, he knows better than anyone else what tin of good-sounding arguments the fox will open. Flup says yes: with reservations. The offer is nice, but it will require a lot of moving out. The Germans want to see him regularly in their heimat, but is physical preparedness still good enough? Baugé - himself once a reasonable pistier - laughs away the arguments and suggests Thys test in the 100-kilometre pair races from October. Due to the influx of riders, Brussels, copied from Paris, will set up qualifiers for the Six Days. Philippe smoothly forces a place. He can still do it.

The six runs from old to new. Philippe is still a rider in 1927, alongside Marcel Boogmans. The townsman is part of a famous Brussels trio. With brother René, he makes the switch to the ovals of the States at a young age, where there are a lot of dollars to be earned at that time. Six-day races are booming business on the US east coast. Sister Fientje Boogmans is Piet Van Kempen's wife. The Dutchman got a stepping stone into the small track world through his sweetheart.

Fientje is his business manager and, with great presence and a big greedy sacoche, steps into the offices of the piste directors without knocking, to collect cash for which hubby has been cycling around. Thys-Boogmans join in, on routine. They get noticed daily and stay on board for 144 hours for a solid classification. Top five would be fantastic and unexpected. Desmedt launches Snel De Gelas - father of later Anderlecht attacker Susse - for the final sprint. They pick up a few points and relegate the Brusselers to sixth place. Baugé can sleep on both ears. Son fils Philippe still has gravy enough in his legs to convince the German directors. There is no turning back. The suitcases for Germany are ready. In spring, the teammates will meet in the Rûtt-Arena. Van Hevel, Vermandel, Sellier, the Debaets brothers, Zanaga, Belloni, Blanchonnet, the black Ibron and some German and Austrian youngsters: an impressive company. Philippe will pocket a lot of Reichsmarks, but must perform. This is also his firm belief. Under no circumstances does he want to be at the start as some kind of creaky attraction. German cycling is strong and yet undervalued in those days. There is talent riding around and a decent calendar of long-distance races. The Kohl brothers, Wolke, Tietz and Huschke can cycle a bit, but are not allowed to prove themselves internationally. There is still a political and sporting embargo in place. Local races fail to gain status. After WWI, the establishments end up in the economic depression and after 1933 they are already looked at askew. They do not get out of isolation. On 22 May, Hanover-Bremen-Hamburg is a hefty drive-in tailored to Van Hevel. In the Harzronde, a week later, Vermandel wins with his fingers in his pockets. Thys is eighth.

There, news trickles in that Bottechia has been found on a country road: beaten up and fighting for his life. The bear will not make it. No one knows exactly what happened to him. Philippe regrets the brawl at Perpignan's neighbourhood school. There is no time to wonder. Erfurt, Leipzig, Berlin ... das gelbe tricot has to compete everywhere. Thys finds the joy again that is needed to make getting off the bike not a habit. In July, he is finally back home.

The Limburg Days Council is a race to maintain fitness, because soon the new heimat will call again. The Riders' friends from Sint Truiden look glum. With 17, they leave for Tongeren. Only the name Thys makes up for it. From Borgloon onwards, there are sharp bits of mountain and Flup gets on the pedals. Thysmans and Dossche follow. Towards Maaskant he is off again, this time with Deschepper and again Thysmans. Through the later mining communities, it's on to Tienen and Diest. Philippe

▲ Stockelynck, Thollembeek and Boogmans

▲ Marcel Boogmans

▲ During the Paris Six Days.

knows he has to keep his last cartouche in his pocket for as long as possible. In Nieuwerkerken, he brings out the hammer, elegantly takes 200 metres and wins his last road race with a good minute's lead over young giant Jef Wauters.

On the piste of Enghien, Philippe comes to cash in on another contract, en route to Normandy's Flers. After the omnium with Van Inghelgem near Camembert, Charles Meurger awaits on the way back, for a final camp in Roubaix. In La douce, the Tour legend is still a household name. Rebry-Thys his start August outstanding at the Maldegem track. In an hour on his own, Thys is once again the best. There will be no wear and tear: gear up and track to Dresden. Flup digests it Wunderbar: because the end is in sight. It is decided. In the orbit around Florence on the Elbe - then curly baroque intact - new Germany sets the tone. Nebe and Remold mouse under and show character. Thys makes a silly slip on the wet stones of the Zaschendörfer Wald and comes back limping. He will have to cancel some clean slope contracts. It is his last year. That is certain, but that is not how farewells are said. In the prickly 1000 Ans Gembloutois, they will have to be of good cheer to follow the old one. With Debaets as company, they push hard on every slope. On the fourth lap, Phillipe pops his tube. He fights back and still closes in sight of the finish line. Still sprinting along is too much. Place seven is not very satisfying. It is no different. At the Belgian Championships in Brasschaat, Thys goes on leave for good. With Mortelmans, Delbecque and Matton, a new generation is on the podium.

There will be no big farewell meeting. Dash below. Tomorrow begins a different life. The triple tour winner has taken all the precautions in his hometown of Anderlecht and becomes a bicycle salesman-garagist. Later, he starts a bus company. On the Chaussée de Mons, a residential block emerges with large garages and offices at the bottom. When in the late summer of 1930 the Jubelstadion (the name Heyzelstadion is from much later) opens, Thys de Mey is also on the roof.

To earn steady income, Philippe bids for the lease of the bus line to the Racecourses with his first Jonckheere bus on Dodge chassis. On board, 23 people can be seated. Horse riding is still popular among Brussels residents. Boitsfort, Dilbeek and Groenendaal, Stokkel and Zellik take turns offering competition afternoons. Le par direct or den tiercé, becomes a veritable capital disease. On zennen trante-e-un (Easter best) or under the canopy of ne gruute chapeau weekly on de Pjeerekoers goen is both frolic and popular entertainment.

Mother died in December 1935 on the eve of St Nicholas. Theo could have put another basket there. It is quiet in the new house. Maman always had to puzzle to raise the offspring. Once Philippe became a top driver, there was no longer a money problem, but a lot of absence. That created more than a mother-child bond. They were allies. Ma had to cope on her own very often and was therefore thoroughly worn out at 64.

In 1936, the first week of congé payé arrives and the desk people already dare to go abroad for a few days. Not too far, because suppose they don't like the food there. Thys's foresight is starting to pay off. He has now also bought a Citroën with more seats and a Wiesse occassion coach from the neighbourhood railways, to expand the scheduled service. Societies on day outings are swapping from along more the train for a rocking bus that picks them up at the door of the venue and drops them off. Philippe still follows cycling a bit from a distance, via Brussels Sportif. When they ask him to wield the gavel, he cannot refuse. But soon busy occupations are invoked to quietly move to an advisor position in the lee. A sighing yes from Thys is occasionally the polite version of a no in sliders. By buying time, he also led his competitors by the nose in the course. That is why the end goal remained no less flawless. Not making direct enemies is sometimes more rewarding than having firm friends.

In 1938, Philippe follows some Tour rides after long insistence. From the back seat, he criticises the systematic splitting of stages and distances, the swerve to neighbouring countries and ever-changing cities. The Tour is losing exceptionality and heroism. Without that, the sport has no future: concludes the record holder hastily. He clings to pioneering times and all too easily represses his otherwise innovative business acumen. Because the ego sports beast in him wants to finally secure the exclusivity of his own achievements? Necessary DNA building blocks to become a top athlete prevent celebrities from pleading for recognition from others and from other times. One has to accept that behind the ballustrade: even from the most cuddly ones.

Years after its introduction, Thys still does not believe in the country formula: it brings no clarity and the team managers are puppets on strings who cannot make decisions. They themselves are not allowed to choose the riders they will go to the Tour with, let alone prepare talent for the stage race.

Flup was once asked to lead the Tour team. When he set conditions, contacts were broken. It leaves him cold. The race has become an afterthought. A fourth vehicle goes on order from his old friends at Opel, a beautiful and comfortable model: the Blitz. The Krieg will soon follow.

1946

On the road

Over the course of February 1946, Thys sits in the stands of the Le Fronton pelota hall to watch the first women's Belgian basketball international. The garish Jai Alai Hall, replete with Basque colours, looks combative. The venue seems chosen mainly to scare the Parisiennes. The fact that the boiler works on ration coupons and does not get cellar coal is not conducive to nice basket. The young Belgian women need that windfall.

Philippe wants to see cousin Joseé, barely 22, at work. The Thys scion plays a sterling game, keeping high jumper Colchen out of the match and allowing the dreaded Arlette Reni to score only 13 times. Belgium surprisingly beat the more mature French team 41-38. A heartwarming sporting moment on the Wavre stone road deserves a chunky demi in the lower town. The race is out of the question now. There is no Tour ahead and other work to do.

Motor coach activity has to be revived after the miserable years of occupation. The scarcity of fuel plays an important role in this too. Picking up an extra bidon essence is the net difference between passing the competition or standing still yourself. Two Parisian newspapers have plans to set up a week-long stage race across France. Actually, that story is hardly about cycling. There is massive political scheming going on behind the scenes, with everyone pulling for the French flag at the loudest. The Communists on the red side, burgeoning Gaullism on the blue. The bad example of the 1919 round trip that Desgrange chased coûte que coûte through a dislocated country is the argument Thys uses everywhere to turn back impatient regulars and forward-thinking journalists. Everyone wants to snack on the Tour de France again as soon as possible. The former winner boldly posits that it cannot yet be done and is not desirable.

The first post-war Tour does not come until 1947 and will be totally dedicated to the Allied victory. New strongman Goddet plays with the idea of putting the limited Dutch cycling nation into a mixed team with Brits. The Dutch are not so keen on merging with left-footed footballers and would rather advocate enlisting in the Foreign Legion.

The press has been speculating for months about who will and will not be there. The round generates enormous enthusiasm. People are eager, craving - after dark years - entertainment and exercise. Bart Lotigiers, the new head of sports at daily newspaper Het Volk, was able to convince the ACV publisher to print an extra evening edition every day. The Tourgazetje is being circulated by street boys in all the neighbourhood.

Monsieur Philippe, still a record man, despite professional pursuits, let himself be talked into following the Tour as an occasional journalist and writing a daily commentary piece. Well and truly contractually agreed, Thys is already at a loss. Who is going to run these things here for a month? Twenty-something Theo lulls that it will work out. Busy times anyway. July is holiday month. The scheduled service, driving working-class children to the sea colony, arranging day trips for local associations who all want to see the waterfalls of Coo and Bastogne. Golden years lie ahead for the travel industry. Flup laments the silly commitment. Yet at the behest of the confident home front, he lets go of his worries and pulls the front door shut behind him. Kubler wins the opening stage to Lille in a hot air oven. The Swiss pays for it the very next day, on the way to Brussels, when René Vietto sets up un solo époustouflant in even more intense heat. The suggestion comes too late, but Marc Sleen - in his debut year - could have drawn - without exaggeration - a sun whose tentacles made the riders' jerseys catch fire.

Brussels' Prosper Depredomme is eager to win in his own city, but reacts too late and, together with Impanis, arrives in den bos (the Bois de la Cambre) a good minute after the Frenchman. Philippe has himself dropped off at home, where they burst into laughter. The next morning, after breakfast, they subtly work him out with: yes yes yes, everything is still under control and now get out of here.

It remains stiflingly hot. On the way to Luxembourg, Thys cannot believe his eyes. Depredomme went deep yesterday and is struggling. Disappointment will play a part. Pros steps off. Philippe slaps his hands on his sticky trousers: whoa, giving

▲ "And why not France, madam, that's a clean country." Philippe Thys knowledgeably provides explanations to clients at his travel agency in Brussels.

up in the national jersey even before the caravan has left your country.... you don't. The record man shifts from left to right on the hot passenger seat. Impanis, also at the front yesterday, barely makes any headway and in turn bemoans the unbearable temperatures. Ray lets it all stick instead of pulling himself together and driving on. A powerful youngster in the prime of his life. He could bloody well take the yellow jersey and au contraire let himself be blown away for 15 minutes: curses Flup again. That the Belgians are retaining heat with their inappropriate black jerseys cannot be a reason. Thys briskly dismisses that drivel: in 1911 we rode the Circuit Français, four full weeks in over 35 degrees, with a heavy rucksack full of equipment on our rable (back). At the end of the third ride, he reaches for the first phone in the Grand Duchy and calls son Theo. The latter frowns at the other end of the line, but the message is clear: come and pick me up in Luxembourg tonight. Asked what is so urgent, Flup replies that he has seen enough and can already write his final article.

Thys no longer wants to understand the pro peloton and irritably disappears from the caravan. He is also rooting his way out of the story a bit cheaply. The facts would prove him wrong and then still a little right. Vietto gets to sleep in yellow every night and dream of final wins. Only in the longest Tour time trial to date, Rene goes head-to-head against Brambilla.

Impanis wins that crono and will make it to the magical Prinsenpark as sixth and by far the best Belgian. So Raymond could pull himself together. Robic eventually wins the Tour: as the leader of the Breton team, which has to lead in uniformly centralist France under équipe de l'Ouest. In the final stage to Paris, he dethrones the Italian. To complete his attack successfully, all the French teams are taken into battle. Brambilla may not win the round. From a sporting point of view, the management could not possibly refuse the Italians participation, even if they had dabbled along the wrong front. But winning the round now, too, was out of the question!

Fachleitner is the inspirer of the final day. He is overwhelmingly the strongest, but why doesn't he go his own way? Does he sound too German? Edouard was also born in Italy, the son of an Austrian who later naturalised as a Frenchman. Blue-blanc-rouge is not on him either.

The resistance is everywhere at the table in liberated France, and to be a Frenchman above suspicion, one must establish genetic bloodlines until 1789. Goddet, partly under pressure from the resistance, continues to refuse any Germanic athlete participation in the round until 1958. In this slavish way, he can purge the politically tarnished L'Auto of 1940, now L'Equipe, once and for all.

1953

King Ottokar's Sceptre

Thys won't let it get to his heart. His hands are more than full. In addition to the bus company, he opens a travel agency on Boulevard Anspach and shuttles back and forth between the heart of Brussels and the depot in Anderlecht. By car, Philippe zips from one foreign country to another. This is increasingly becoming his thing. He is always on the road and yet at home everywhere.

Wasn't that artful attitude to life also the supreme test of the sporting success he achieved? Even back then, he could quietly ground, eat and sleep anywhere. With his wife, he visits all the hotels where his clients will stay, negotiating prices and meals, fixing rooms and tasting the local cuisine beforehand. At the Hotel de Rome in Paris, the couple are regulars. Philippe regularly visits his niece there, a close friend of Maurice Chevalier. Years pass in a batty vacances éternelles feeling. Une vie soigneusement gérée avec bon sens, remains Thys's life motto. Hanging around idly and growing old in retirement? He cannot think of that. Theo the coaches and staff, the Godfather de public relations. This is how things have been running within the company for some time.

The firm has full order books: the posh city madam in a summer hat is keen to head for the Côte d' Azur, the young dashing footballers dream of feeling Paris and the

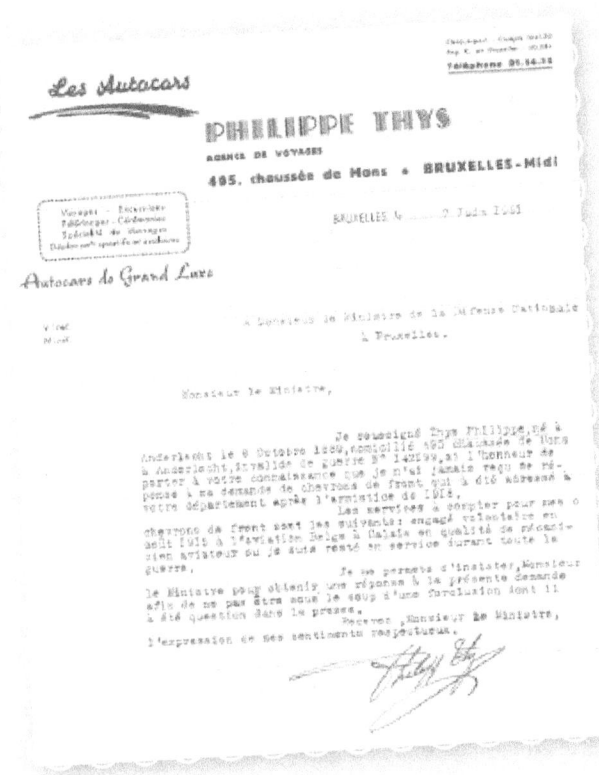

pigeon club wants to fly out for a change. Flup and Theo offer customisation: there are vayoges and vayoges of a day. It's puzzle work to keep everyone a customer. Not to mention the resident groups of the Faubourgs, the savings banks of the staminées and the trade and butchers' shops. That calandeeze wants to go on an outing - me den 21 ste or with half-harvest, the preferance - but without having to sleep in a strange bed, because the shop has to be open tomorrow. The till is permanently ringing on the Chaussée de Mons, even if it is sometimes small tips and hard-earned pennies.

Eagle Eye Thys, has developed - like a good bottle of gueuze - over the years into a round-bodied product. All the signs of age have been transformed into refined sugars. It does not lose its good humour. This is necessary, as buses still break down regularly and communication runs only along thin wires connecting sparse fixed devices. Distances take up a lot of time.

Trails of necessity dock on narrow nationals with crawling vans, often over cobblestones and crossing town centres. Only towards the coast is there a strip of motorway. Many Brussels residents abandon this investment and take the train to the sea.

Less and less time is made for cycling. Only when Van Hammée lui même or Jean Van Buggenhout really insist, does he still sometimes come to the sports palace, to fill their show and spend a few seconds in the hot spotlight. Van Hauwaert - with bicycle factory in Groot Bijgaarden - is the only former colleague he still keeps in regular contact with. Cyrille has a nice villa retreat in Zellik with gorgeous pelouse. If Flup crosses a course somewhere in the Zenne Valley, he will sometimes get out and e klapke doeng, long enough to stay informed and pocket new names. Time to stay till the floral gift he rarely, if ever, has. Following up results is done through the newspaper. In 1953, he gladly accepts the invitation to the lavish ceremony the birthday Tour is putting on. He'd like to see them again, all those sackless bastards. How fat have their bellies grown by now?

Goddet has all available old bicycles and vehicles brought in and dresses everyone in belle-époque attire. The reunion is cordial, but Thys has absolutely no desire for a les copains d'abord atmosphere, never had any. Vague agreements are made, like at all reunions where the wine is more than excellent and drinks away too quickly. The day after, the fun misery is already behind him: an appointment awaits in Anderlecht.

▲ An inscription on a Brussels facade recalls its glorious occupant.

Bobet wins that 50th Tour and is poised to match Thys two years later. With a win in the Tour of Flanders and a third place in Paris-Roubaix, Louison is already top in the spring of 1955. He wears the world jersey and is full of confidence. Final wins in the Tour de Luxembourg and the Dauphiné bring the goal ever closer. It is precisely in the stage to Namur, over the cobblestones of the North, that the Breton shows he is ready. Anyone who can win on his least favourite Tour terrain must be super. Philippe does not fear. He already knows then that it will end in shared glory.

Every day, everywhere he shows up, he gets the same question: will Bobet match your record ... From Namur to Metz, nine riders ride away, including one Antonin Rolland. In the Alps, despite all predictions, the outsider does not go down. In fact, he barely loses time and gets the lead. Bobet has to watch out.

Over the Ventoux, Breton makes up time and there remains the Pyrenees to put things right. Hellish saddle pains shake the plan. Bobet's sensitive skin is playing up. Outstanding form keeps him on the bike. To Saint Gaudens, Rolland will capitulate. Brankart still wins over Tourmalet and Aubisque and in the long time trial. Jean gets to a good five minutes in the standings, but the Frenchman endures fiendish misery and stinging discomfort until Paris. He hoists himself into the annals of the Tour alongside Thys.

A back surgery followed in which a kind of gangrene was cut away, millimetres away from vital organs. Bobet will confess afterwards that riding out Tour 55 on drastic medication had dreadfully undermined his constitution. No war breaks out in 1956 and Thys has to prepare for the worst. But Bobet no longer wins. Fragile and already cycled past by new French talent, he often has to renounce long stage races. The consequences of his urge to still hoist a third Tour victory on board under bad fortune has made further top-level racing impossible.

Anquetil might soon and unceremoniously knock Thys off the throne with his clicking and clacking. It no longer touches Philippe's cold clothes. Against Jacques' contested riding, Philippe does not want to appeal. Should the flamboyant Normand be accused of fighting with his head as often as with his legs? In any case, that accusation could never sound credible or mean from Thys's mouth. Meanwhile, in 1958, the party pigs are let loose once more. Numerous Belgian round winners toured the Expo site in open cars. The marriage between the World Expo and the Tour start in Brussels, then takes place in Old Belgium, a village of wood and plaster where it is fairground for six months. Customers don't wait. Thys must already be heading for Alsace, Black Forest, Switzerland or Alps. On trips abroad, things are already more convivial. Lost driving with him as convoyeur remains limited. Flup has travelled all these stone roads by bike before and behind every bend there is a wonderful story that either amazes or makes the whole bus laugh. In Flemish and French. His customers still ride through the France where roads rest on their medieval coffrage and bump through the front doors of tiny Mairies. On today's wide-open roundabouts around villages, grain still wavers then.

Problems are there along the way every day. They are there to be solved. There is troublesome customs staff, the flush of confrontational German toilet bowls, the treachery of punishing local drinks or the nasty mouthfeel of steaming andouillette. With extremely skilful manipulation of foreign currency, good travellers sometimes want to be fooled. For many, the foreign is still to be taken very literally. Business adapts and seeks new markets. Schools are driven to den bain and diners de chasse fill the empty autumn.

In 1960, while travelling in Nice, Philippe suffered a stomach haemorrhage. The operation and rehabilitation on site take several months. It is time for a change of pace. The birth of a grandson helps him recover. The apple of his eye is called Philippe: someone continues the name. Bompa is over the moon. Business along the overcrowded Chausée de Mons, where buses always struggle to get in and out, passes entirely to son Theo. Flup lives on the first floor. He descends the stairs less frequently. Suddenly all his memorabilia, out of garage storage and out of the house. Pieces lying in dusty boxes, he does not throw away or hand out, neither does he really cherish them and shine them up. It is unfortunate that some unique documents disappeared after a burglary. A copy of L' Auto among others, on which all the top players of the time had signed. The Paris Sports Museum, just founded by friend Jean Durry, is the perfect final destination.

In France they will take care of it, better than here, Thys let slip. Old man fear that it would be carelessly handled after his death? Flup had no reason to suppose so. But if he is convinced of something, it will happen that way. A museum can best guard good preservation, so things are transferred with its own hands.

Thys-Bobet should be off the tables. 1961, 1962, ... Anquetil quickly comes in at three and he is overwhelmingly just the passage. Perhaps it is time to revamp the honours list: now that branded teams are once again calling the shots, legendary cols have been given asphalt comfort and live television pictures are changing the course of the race. Even the old Parc des Princes will have to make way. Plans for a Boulevard pérephérique de Paris are becoming concrete.

Cycling spurted into a new era, totally different from the Thys era. Every year, les Cars Thys put in a trip to the Tour arrival in Paris. It is a success number, for which they have the ticket cutter of choice. So on Saturday 13 July 1963, with some certainty, Philippe rides into his final dethronement. Monsieur Crono won Paris-Nice, the Criterium National, the Vuelta and the Dauphiné that spring. Goddet and Levitan still rushed to the aid of Thys and Bobet, pushing the Tour kilometres against the clock. Will that stop the human machine?

Spaniards are not all-rounders, Poulidor is young and in the hands of a naive commuter, Gaul, Nencini and Bahamontes are experienced but old. Are they still starting this year? Miraculously, it is the black curly-haired Toledo rider who takes the lead on the flat. Anquetil enters the first time trial and then surprisingly wins the stage over the Tourmalet. He climbs better than ever and passes the Spaniard in the classification. The Alpine menu is tough. Bahomontes has to go for it. He takes the yellow in Val d'Isère. Chances and cols abound, but his old knuckles are blocking. Deepening the gap does not succeed. Over the steep Forclaz, ride of last chance, Crazy Gem

- via a bypass of the regulations - puts the course in the fold. Anquetil feigns bad luck and his linky sports director hands over a new light bike with supersized pions on the rear block. Bahamontes cannot throw the Frenchman off and even prevent him from grabbing the stage and bonification as well. Les jeux sont faits, as there is still the luxury of the long time trial.

From the main grandstand, Philippe sees a herd of Belgians dive into the track and launch doggedly into the final sprint. Van Looy then beats Beheyt after all. The yellow leisurely does the obligatory lap and finished. Thys shakes hands with charming Jacques chaleurely, without regret. He is relieved. Now those pesky questions will finally stop. That autumn, the bicycle on which he still occasionally tours the streets of Anderlecht goes by the wayside. Mother the wife must be strict. Elders no longer belong on a bicycle amid the increasingly busy city traffic. Tut...tut...tut: not even when they once won the Tour. What the hell. A new victory king has risen. Anquetil m'a passé, donc, ça ne vaut plus la peine de m'entrainer: jokes Thys. Sitting still is still not an option. Pampering the grandson is. He is constantly allowed to come along on outings. Every day, if mummy lets him. Philippe I doesn't lie awake every day because of the race and doesn't want to force anything on anyone, but... Isn't there a rider in the apple of his eye?

Philippe II gets to pick clean new bikes all the time. Ex-racing bike shops that welcome the palm-fast and chatty duo with open arms are plentiful in the area. Mecano par excellence, Charelke Terryn in rue Birmingham or a few houses down the stone road, Den Hollander, Jef Dominicus and his singing daughter Tonia. Grandson lief, however, does not get the hang of it and son Theo gets irritated: arrête de gâter le gamin. The little one has chronic respiratory problems. Son and daughter-in-law move to the healthy outdoors of Beersel.

That leaves a void at the bus station. Thys is tired, leaves his car in the stable more often and suffers a minor stroke when he returns from a corpse service in the biting cold. A telling sign. Old friends still come to the house: Swiss jewellers, French and German businessmen from inside and outside cycling, friends from somewhere along the way. They are always well received, thanks to the cooking skills of the daughter-in-law. On the set table of the salle à manger comes ripe Alsace, robust Burgundy and soft Armagnac. For the first time in his life, Thys has to take it easy. The exploits of Belgian god and half-Brusselsman Eddy fascinate him. He meets Merckx several more times, gives encouragement and consigns against charlatans and underachievers. But the public forum, crowds and outings are avoided.

On his 80e birthday, Philippe received the latest racing model from the racing stable as a gift from former employer Peugeot, in the yellow colours of the time, custom-made. This brings him joy. The assembled family gives him a big push at the Chau-sée de Mons towards the canal bridge around the corner. Thys shouts after: da Merckx should now hold on to the branches of the buume. Less than a minute later he is back there, emotional and almost weeping because of the beautiful gift. But Flup is not satisfied with his performance and dismounting, he puffs: "Isn't it strange that I once climbed so many cols one after the other and now I can't even get up the light start of the bridge ...

The escape from impermanence is pretty much his last active act. The holy fire goes out faster than expected. The mighty man falls comically silent. He no longer leaves his seat and falls asleep during live cycling broadcasts. Shortly after New Year 1971, he feels really unwell. Heart problems. He gives up, no longer wants to fight. Hospital visits are not welcome. Que on me fou la paix, I was allowed to experience everything, even more than that: is the cool justification of his final abandonment. For a moment more he looks back, at a fascinating life in which he has very rarely had to say merci, visited everywhere and met le beau monde. What other Cureghem-mchançard has had that unexpected opportunity? With varying material, he did the same thing every day for his life: for a fee, cover distances quickly and safely and sell mere mortals a touch of illusion.

After barely a few days of hospitalisation at the Clinique Saint Anne, Philippe Thys dies on Sunday 17 January 1971 before days council. The former Tour record holder did not witness his dethroning by compatriot Merckx. The latter came to offer a farewell greeting in the funeral chapel at his home the morning of his funeral. The busy brick road closes to all traffic for a very short time. Thys is given general right of way for his last stage and a crowd from home and abroad comes to bid him farewell. Cyrille Van Hauwaert is the only one of their generation still standing at the grave, whispering trembling adieu. No speeches. No fuss. Extra corbillards carry flowers and wreaths. Thys had a trademark of always receiving them quietly and peacefully.

▲ On a stage in front of Paris City Hall, the greatest Tour legends are honored. From left to right: Louison Bobet (1953 & 1955), Hugo Koblet (1951), Ferdinand Kubler (1950), Jean Robic (1947), Gino Bartali (1938), Roger Lapébie (1937), Nicolas Frantz (1927 & 1928), Eugène Christophe (3rd in 1919), Lucien Buysse (1926), Firmin Lambot (1919), Philippe Thys (1913, 1914 et 1920).

Palmares

Philippe Thys

Date of birth: **08-10-1889**
Place of birth: **Anderlecht (Brussels-Capital Region), Belgium**
Died: **17-01-1971**
Place of death: **Anderlecht (Brussels Capital Region),
Belgium**Professional cyclist from 1912 to 1927

Victories

Total: **26**

Track - Six-days races: **1**

Cross-country - National Champion: **1**

Classification - Road - Final

Classification: **4**

Road - Stage: **12**

Road - Couple Time Trial: **1**

Road - Contest: **7**

Victories by team/year:

1911: **1**

1912: **0**

1913: **2**

1914: **3**

1915: **0**

1916: **0**

1917: **2**

1918: **1**

1919: **1**

1920: **5**

1921: **1**

1922: **6**

1923: **1**

1924: **1**

1925: **0**

1926: **0**

1927: **1**

Teams

1911   Independent (Unknown)
1912   Peugeot - Wolber (France)
1913   Peugeot - Wolber (France)
1914   Peugeot - Wolber (France)
1915   Individueel (Onbekend)
1916   Individueel (Onbekend)
1917   Peugeot - Wolber (Belgium)
1918   Peugeot - Wolber (Belgium)
1919   La Sportive (France)
1920   La Sportive (France)
1921   Stucchi - Pirelli (Italy)
1921   Pirelli (Belgium)
1921   La Sportive (France)
1922   Peugeot - Wolber (France)
1923   Peugeot - Wolber (France)
1924   Peugeot - Wolber (France)
1925   Automoto - Hutchinson (France)
1926   Individueel (Onbekend)
1927   Opel - ZR III (Germany)

Complete Palmares

1908   2nd in Tour de Limburg, Amateurs, Belgium

1909   2nd in Antwerp - Menin, Belgium
1909   13rd in Liège - Bastogne - Liège, Belgium

1910   3rd in Charleroi (Etoile Caroloregienne) , Belgium
1910   1st in National Championship, Cross-country, Elite, Belgium,

1911   1st in Final ranking Tour de France des Indépendants
        (Circuit Français Peugeot) , France

1912   6th in Final ranking Tour de France (Tour de France)

1913   1st in 6e etappe (Tour de France) , Luchon
1913   3rd in 7e etappe (Tour de France) , Perpignan
1913   3rd in 9e etappe (Tour de France) , Nice
1913   3rd in 10e etappe (Tour de France) , Grenoble
1913   3rd in 11st etappe (Tour de France) , Genève
1913   1st in Final ranking (Tour de France)

1914   1st in Paris - Menin (Parijs - Menen) , Belgium
1914   3rd in Paris - Tours, Tours (Centre), France
1914   1st in 1st etappe (Tour de France) , Le Havre
1914   2nd in 2nd etappe (Tour de France) , Cherbourg
1914   3rd in 5e etappe (Tour de France) , Bayonne
1914   2nd in 6e etappe (Tour de France) , Luchon
1914   3rd in 7e etappe (Tour de France) , Perpignan
1914   3rd in 9e etappe (Tour de France) , Nice
1914   3rd in 11st etappe (Tour de France) , Genève
1914   3rd in 14e etappe (Tour de France) , Dunkerque
1914   1st in Final ranking (Tour de France)

1917   1st in Paris - Tours, Tours (Centre), France

1917   1st in Giro di Lombardia (Il Lombardia) , Italy

1918   1st in Tours - Paris (Blois - Chaville) , France

1919   1st in Brussel/Bruxelles, Six-days, Belgium + Marcel Dupuy

1919   2nd in Paris - Roubaix, Roubaix (Nord-Pas-de-Calais), France

1920   3rd in 1st etappe (Tour de France) , Le Havre

1920   1st in 2nd etappe (Tour de France) , Cherbourg

1920   2nd in 4e etappe (Tour de France) , Les Sables-d'Olonne

1920   2nd in 5e etappe (Tour de France) , Bayonne

1920   2nd in 6e etappe (Tour de France) , Luchon

1920   2nd in 7e etappe (Tour de France) , Perpignan

1920   2nd in 8e etappe (Tour de France) , Aix-en-Provence

1920   1st in 9e etappe (Tour de France) , Nice

1920   1st in 12nd etappe (Tour de France) , Strasbourg

1920   1st in 13rd etappe (Tour de France) , Metz

1920   2nd in 14e etappe (Tour de France) , Dunkerque

1920   2nd in 15e etappe (Tour de France) , Paris

1920   1st in Final ranking (Tour de France)

1921   1st (+Rossius) Parijs-Dijon (= G.P.Sporting)

1921   2nd in Final ranking Giro della Provincia Milano (b), Italy

1921   1st in Critérium des As, France

1921   3rd in Bordeaux - Paris, France

1922   2nd in National Championship, Op de weg, Elite, Belgium, Spa

1922   1st in Paris - Lyon (GP Sporting) , France met Jean Alavoine

1922   2nd in 2nd etappe (Tour de France) , Cherbourg

1922   1st in 4e etappe (Tour de France) , Les Sables-d'Olonne

1922   1st in 8e etappe (Tour de France) , Toulon

1922   1st in 9e etappe (Tour de France) , Nice

1922   1st in 10e etappe (Tour de France) , Briançon

1922   3rd in 13rd etappe (Tour de France) , Metz

1922   1st in 15e etappe (Tour de France) , Paris

1922   14e in Final ranking (Tour de France)

1923   1st in Paris - Lyon (GP Sporting) , France
       with Jean Alavoine and Nicolas Frantz
1923   3rd in 4th stage of Tour de France, Les Sables-d'Olonne

1924   2nd in 3rd etappe (Tour de France) , Brest
1924   2nd in 7e etappe (Tour de France) , Perpignan
1924   1st in 9e etappe (Tour de France) , Nice
1924   11st in Final ranking (Tour de France)

1925   3rd in Brussel/Bruxelles, Six-days, Belgium

1927   1st in Sint-Truiden (Limburgse Dageraad) (Limburg), Belgium

Ranking victories
Tour de France

5 victories

Jacques Anquetil 1957, 1961, 1962, 1963, 1964
Eddy Merckx 1969, 1970, 1971, 1972, 1974
Bernard Hinault 1978, 1979, 1981, 1982, 1985
Miguel Indurain 1991, 1992, 1993, 1994, 1995

4 victories

Chris Froome 2013, 2015, 2016, 2017

3 victories

Philippe Thys 1913, 1914, 1920
Louison Bobet 1953, 1954, 1955
Greg LeMond 1986, 1989, 1990

2 victories

Lucien Petit-Breton 1907, 1908
Firmin Lambot 1919, 1922
Ottavio Bottecchia 1924, 1925
Nicolas Frantz 1927, 1928
André Leducq 1930, 1932
Antonin Magne 1931, 1934
Sylvère Maes 1936, 1939
Gino Bartali 1938, 1948
Fausto Coppi 1949, 1952
Bernard Thévenet 1975, 1977
Laurent Fignon 1983, 1984
Alberto Contador 2007, 2009
Tadej Pogacar 2020, 2021
Jonas Vingegaard 2022, 2023

À Charles Aerts
Bien Cordialement en souvenir
de mes Victoires dans les Tours de France
1911-13-14-20